JESUS
WAS A
BILLIONAIRE

BREAKING THE CURSE OF BEING BROKE

ALLAN SEALY

LIFE AND SUCCESS PUBLISHING
www.abookinsideyou.com

Life and Success Media Ltd
email info@abookinsideyou.com
www.abookinsideyou.com

ISBN: 978-1-7398859-7-7

Cover design & layout by
miadesign.com

CONTENTS

CONTENTS

CONTENTS

DEDICATION

This Book is dedicated to
my daughters, Jasmin & Jada.
I love you both deeply.

SPECIAL THANKS

I want to give special thanks to:

My Dad (The Wise One)
- for your wisdom, love and guidance -

My Mother (My Rock)
- for your unfailing love and sacrifice -

SUPREME THANKS

My supreme thanks to:

My Heavenly Father,
The Lord Jesus Christ
& The Holy Spirit

through whom all things are possible

PART 1

YOUNG GIFTED AND RICH

———◆———

FOREWORD

THE REAL JESUS CHRIST

The common concept of Christ was given to the church by the priests of the dark ages, at a time when a religious ideal was wanted which should induce men to be content with slavery, and to bow their necks to every kind of wrong and oppression; and this concept was drawn almost wholly from the poetry of Isaiah; the Christ of the churches is the Christ of Isaiah, and our ideas of Him are not drawn at all from an impartial study of the history of His life. Such passages in the prophecies as; *"He is despised and rejected of men; a man of sorrows and acquainted with grief; and we hid, as it were, our faces from him; he is brought as a lamb to the slaughter, and as a sheep before her shearers is dumb, so he opened not his mouth,"* have been quoted to show His character, and the meekness and humbly submissive spirit with which He endured wrong and injustice. We have had held up as the ideal man a despised, friendless, poverty-stricken laborer whom the upper classes regarded with scorn because of his lowly origin and station; who had no friends save fishermen, laborers, outcasts and sinners; who was often shirtless and hungry, and who bore insults and persecutions with meek submission, and walked about in a scornful world with his hands always uplifted in loving benediction.

This character has too long been offered as the Christian ideal;

- Be meek,
- Be submissive,
- Be lamb-like or sheep-like.

Bow your head before the persecutor, and offer your back to the shearer. Rejoice when you are fleeced; it is for the glory of God. It is a good religion *for the man with the shears.*

The Christ who was held up in the old-fashioned orthodox pulpit is a weak character. He is not the kind of a man we would nominate for president, and his followers have very little faith in Him as an organizer. No railroad magnate of today would make Him foreman of a section; and if it were broadcast over the country tonight that the president of the United States had resigned and that Jesus would be inaugurated tomorrow, 95 percent of the Christians there would draw their money out of the banks for fear Jesus might start a panic.

What we propose to do now is to ascertain by a study of the four gospels in the light of history whether this is the real Christ; and if not, to find what the real Christ was like.

In the first place, Jesus could not have been despised because He was a carpenter, or the reputed son of a carpenter. Custom required every Jewish Rabbi or teacher to have a trade. We read in the Talmud of Rabbi Johanan, the blacksmith, and of Rabbi Isaac, the shoemaker, learned and highly honored men. Rabbi Jesus, the carpenter, would be spoken of in the same way. St. Paul, a very learned man, was a tent-maker by trade. At that time, and among that people, Jesus could not have been despised for His birth and station. He was popularly supposed to be of royal blood, being saluted as the son of David; His lineage was well known. The people who cried *"Hosannah to the son of David"* knew that He was an aristocrat of the aristocrats; a prince of the royal house. He was not *"lowly"* in birth, nor was He supposed to be so.

HE WAS EDUCATED

Second, He could not have been despised for His ignorance, for He was a very learned man. Whenever He went into a synagogue, He was selected to read the law and teach the congregation, as the one best qualified for that work. Luke says; *"There went a fame of Him through all the region round about, and He taught in their synagogues, being glorified of all."* In those times of fierce religious disputation, no unlearned man could have held his own in such fashion. He must have been letter-perfect in the books of the Jewish law, for He was always able to rout His adversaries by making apt quotations from their own books. Even His enemies always addressed Him as Master, or Teacher, acknowledging His profound learning.

JESUS HAD PLENTY

Third, He was not despised for His poverty, for He had many wealthy and influential friends, and knew no lack of anything. Lazarus and his sisters, whose home was always open to Him, were people of consequence; for we are told that *"many of the Jews"* came to comfort the sisters when Lazarus died.

Luke says that Joanna, the wife of Chuza, the king's steward, and other women *"ministered unto him of their substance;"* that is, they were supporters of His work.

The king's steward was a high official, and his wife would be a prominent lady.

Joseph of Arimathea, who came to get the body of Jesus, was a well-to-do man. So, probably was Nicodemus.

Jesus healed the sick in the families of rulers and high officials, and they appear to have responded liberally in supplying His financial needs.

He dressed expensively, lived well and never lacked for money. When He was crucified, the soldiers cast lots for His clothing because it was too fine to cut up, as they would have done with the garments of an ordinary man; and on the night of His betrayal, when Judas went out, it was supposed by the others that he had gone to give something to the poor. It must have been their custom to give away money, or how could such a supposition have arisen?

In that country and climate, the wants of Jesus and His disciples were few and simple, and they seem to have been fully supplied. He wore fine clothes, had plenty to eat and drink, and had money to give away.

JESUS WAS NOT HUMBLE

Fourth, Jesus was not humble, in the *commonly accepted* meaning of the word. He was a man of the most impressive, commanding and powerful personal appearance. He *"spoke as one having authority"* and *"His word was with power."*

Frequently, we are told, great fear and awe fell upon the people at His mighty words and works. In one place they were so frightened that they besought Him to leave; and John tells how certain officers sent to arrest Him in the market place lost their nerve in His commanding presence, and went back, saying *"Surely, never man spake like this man."*

On the night of His arrest a band of soldiers approached Him in the grove and asked for Jesus of Nazareth; and when He answered "I am he," such was His majesty and power that they prostrated themselves; "they went backward," the account says, "and fell to the ground."

- John 18:6

To be like the Christ of the four Gospels, one must be learned, well dressed, well supplied with money, and of noble and commanding appearance, speaking with authority, and having tremendous magnetic power.

Wallace Wattles
Author of The Science of Getting Rich

CHAPTER 1

GOD VS MONEY

"No one can serve two masters; for either he will hate the one and love the other"

I n 1867, Charles Spurgeon *(known as the 'prince of preachers')*, delivering a sermon to the then largest church congregation in Christendom, said,

"I believe that it is anti-Christian and unholy for any Christian to live with the object of accumulating wealth. You will say, 'Are we not to strive all we can to get all the money we can?' You may do so. I cannot doubt but what, in so doing, you may do service to the cause of God. But what I said was that to live with the object of accumulating wealth is anti-Christian."

Saint Josemaria Escriva, founder of the Catholic organization - Opus Dei, was asked in an interview to comment on the virtue of poverty in view of increasing social awareness in society. Here is an excerpt from what he said,

"The poor will have the Gospel preached to them' (Matthew 11:6).

We read in Scripture, precisely as one of the signs which mark the arrival of the Kingdom of God. Those who do not love and practice the virtue of poverty do not have Christ's spirit. This holds true for everyone. For the hermit who retires to the desert; and for the ordinary Christian who lives among his fellow men, whether he enjoys the use of this world's resources or is short of many of them."

St. Augustine's doctrine of charity became the heart of Christian thought and practice. Augustine portrayed the Christian pilgrimage toward the heavenly city by analogy to a traveler's journey home.

"The city of God, humankind's true home, is characterized by the love of God even to the contempt of self, whereas the earthly city is characterized by the love of self even to the contempt of God. It is the goal—not the journey—that is important. The world and its goods may be used for the journey, but if they are enjoyed, they direct the traveler away from God to the earth."

So I ask you…

"IS IT GREEDY OR ANTI-CHRISTIAN TO EARN MUCH MORE THAN YOU (AND YOUR FAMILY) NEED TO LIVE ON?"

"IS IT REALLY AGAINST THE SPIRIT OF CHRIST NOT TO PRACTICE THE VIRTUE OF POVERTY?"

"WOULD THE ENJOYMENT OF MATERIAL WEALTH REALLY STEER YOU AWAY FROM GOD?"

Although these questions have a moral value attached to them, ultimately, they are derived from a particular perception concerning God and money. As a result, there is a great amount of ambivalence within the church, on the subject of money and the possession of material wealth. So much so, that Christianity seems to be polarized into two main camps:

Those who are hyper-prosperity, believing that being prosperous is the only sign of God's favor and blessings on one's life.

Versus

Those who consider the theology of prosperity to be the most damnable heresies in the history of the Church.

Amongst the middle ground are those who although are not anti-prosperity, believe in a prosperity with a *low* glass ceiling!

So, who's right? Who's wrong? More importantly, who has God's divine stamp of approval? To address this issue, let's talk about mammon.

MAMMON

"No one can serve two masters; for either he will hate the one and love the other, or else he will be loyal to the one and despise the other. You cannot serve God and mammon."

- Matthew 6:24

Although mammon is often used to refer to 'money,' 'the personification of money,' or in extreme cases, *'the demon spirit of money,'* generally speaking, mammon pertains to the *influence* of money. Influence, by definition, is the capacity to affect the character, development, or behavior of someone. That being the case, mammon is more *mental* than physical. The physical counterpart of money has no intrinsic value. It is just cheap paper and metal coins. Its value only lies in it being an 'accepted' medium of exchange for goods, services, and time. That acceptance is the *conscious* part of money, which is where its influence lies. From now on, when the words money or mammon are mentioned in this book, I want to you to think of it as a **form of influence**.

Prior to saying you cannot serve God and mammon, Jesus shared the story of the *'unjust steward,'* setting the tone and context for His statement about money.

"There was a certain rich man who had a steward, and an accusation was brought to him that this man was wasting his goods. So he

called him and said to him, 'What is this I hear about you? Give an account of your stewardship, for you can no longer be steward.' Then the steward said within himself, 'What shall I do? For my master is taking the stewardship away from me. I cannot dig; I am ashamed to beg. I have resolved what to do, that when I am put out of the stewardship, they may receive me into their houses.'

So, he called every one of his master's debtors to him, and said to the first, 'How much do you owe my master?' And he said, 'A hundred measures of oil.' So he said to him, 'Take your bill, and sit down quickly and write fifty.' Then he said to another, 'And how much do you owe?' So he said, 'A hundred measures of wheat.' And he said to him, 'Take your bill, and write eighty.' So the master commended the unjust steward because he had dealt shrewdly. For the sons of this world are more shrewd in their generation than the sons of light.

*And I say to you, make friends for yourselves by **unrighteous mammon**, that when you fail, they may receive you into an everlasting home. He who is faithful in what is least is faithful also in much; and he who is unjust in what is least is unjust also in much. Therefore, if you have not been faithful in the unrighteous mammon, who will commit to your trust the true riches?*

- Luke 16:1-11

Although Jesus described mammon as 'unrighteous,' He whole-heartedly endorsed the use of it! This sentiment is reflected in the case of the 'unjust steward,' who under the threat of losing his livelihood, used the influence of money for the future betterment of himself, and as it turned out, the betterment of his employer. Not only was the steward commended for his actions, but his handling of 'unrighteous mammon' served as an example of why,

"The children of this world are in their generation wiser than the children of light."

- Luke 16:8 KJV

"BUT WHY WOULD JESUS ENDORSE THE USE OF SOMETHING HE CALLS UNRIGHTEOUSNESS?"

To answer this question, let us first define what righteousness is. Righteousness is a complex word with multiple definitions and usages. These definitions include:

- The quality of being morally right or justifiable
- To act according to moral or divine law
- To be free from guilt or sin
- To make right decisions
- Doing what is right
- The quality of being right in God's eyes

I believe a more concise meaning can be gained using the principle of *first mention.* According to Biblical hermeneutics *(the science of interpreting ancient text)*, when an important word or concept occurs for the first time in the Bible, the context in which it is used sets the pattern for its primary usage and development all throughout the Scriptures. The first time 'righteousness' is mentioned in the Bible was when Abraham believed in God, based on the vision He received from Him.

"Look now toward heaven, and count the stars if you are able to number them." And He said to him, "So shall your descendants be." And he [Abraham] believed in the Lord, and He accounted it to him for righteousness.

- Genesis 15:5-6

Righteousness, in its simplest form, is *believing* God. More specifically, believing in the divine revelation of your *who you truly are!* Although Abraham had no heir, he believed in the God-given vision of being the *'father of many nations,'* and this was counted onto him as righteousness. From that point onward, Abraham's **self-image** was transformed according to the vision given to him by God. In many cases, a divine revelation is for the ultimate purpose of self-revelation - setting you on a path where you are divinely connected to the people, resources, and opportunities required to fulfill your purpose and manifest *the person* God created you to be.

Therefore, what makes mammon 'unrighteous' *(especially in large quantities)* is because it is a means of obtaining almost anything you want, void of **discovering your true self.** Righteousness, on the other hand, empowers you to manifest the good that you desire from a position of understanding your **Divine Identity.**

There is also a tendency for those who believe they can buy whatever they want to put their confidence in money and in *'materiality,'* rather than in God. However, as will be covered later in this book, this is but another example of living a life void of understanding your true self.

BUY WITHOUT MONEY

The Righteous, therefore, manifest the good that they desire from the understanding of who God created them to be. Although many believe that the good that they desire can only be obtained by money, those who understand righteousness **buy without money!**

Everyone who thirsts, come to the waters; and you who have no money, come, buy and eat. Yes, come, buy wine and milk without money and without price.

- Isaiah 55:1

HOW CAN ONE BUY WITHOUT MONEY?

On the surface, this may seem absurd; however, buying without money is a powerful spiritual principle that every living person on the planet can deploy! Moreover, as I will explain later in this book, buying without money is integral to the *gospel of Christ*. The good news of a spiritual Kingdom of unlimited resources and power, by which one can obtain whatever they desire *if they believe.*

SERVING TWO MASTERS

Despite the fact we are to buy without money, Jesus tells us to be *faithful* with the unrighteous mammon, and God keeps *providing* ways for us to have more of it in our pockets! No wonder there is so much ambivalence on the subject of God and money! To address this issue and hopefully resolve the *perceived* animosity between God and money, let us carefully examine Jesus' statement regarding God and mammon.

"No one can serve two masters; for either he will hate the one and love the other, or else he will be loyal to the one and despise the other. You cannot serve God and mammon."

- Luke 16:13

At first glance, it looks like Jesus is saying,

"Money is the enemy and God's biggest rival."

"You cannot serve two masters, so you must choose between God and money."

"Your antipathy for money is proof of your love and devotion to God."

"Those who desire to be rich, have taken their side against God."
"Your choice in this matter will determine your eternal destiny!"

This is the sentiment of many who believe that money is the *root of all evil!*

ALTHOUGH, MONEY IS OFTEN USED TO CIRCUMVENT THE NEED FOR GOD, DOES THAT MEAN WE CANNOT HAVE BOTH GOD AND MONEY?

First of all, money *is not* the root of all evil. Only the *love* of it is *(1 Timothy 6:10)*. Second, Jesus did not say you cannot have God and mammon, He said you cannot *serve* God and mammon. This is a very important distinction. Money is a resource and a tool, nothing more, nothing less! It is not something you should either love or hate! If you pay attention to what Jesus is saying you will understand that when it comes to God and money, *loving one and hating the other*, or *being loyal to one and despising the other* is the consequence of serving two masters! The person whose love for God is *defined* by their hatred towards money *(and those who have it)* is in the same boat as the person whose love for money defines their animosity towards God. Knowingly or not, *both are serving two masters!*

To be clear, I am not saying you should not have any convictions in regard to riches gained by greed, corruption, or unlawful practices. What I am saying is,

"If your love or hatred towards money defines your relationship with God, you are serving two masters."

The perceived conflict between God and money is as ridiculous as a conflict between the heavyweight, boxing champion of the world and an ant! No one would ever consider such a fight. However, imagine if such a bout were organized, and there was heavy betting on the ant to win! For this to be remotely possible, there has to be a perception of a phenomenally magnified ant or a severely diminished boxing champion! As nonsensical as this notion sounds, how much more absurd is it to compare God with money?

Although God has no equal, whatever you compare to God is either deified or magnified!

•

God does not want you to love or hate money.

•

God wants you to be trustworthy enough to have plenty
of money for your own benefit and the benefit of others.

•

You can have as much money as you need or desire
as long as money does not have you!

•

Money will either be your hardworking slave
or your brutal master. It is in your power to
determine which it will be.

*"Every gold piece you save is a slave to work for you.
Every copper it earns is its child that can also earn for you."*

*"You do eat the children of your savings,
then how do you expect them to work for you?
And how can they have children that will also work for you?"*

- George S. Clason's book, The Richest Man in Babylon.

CHAPTER 2

CHRIST VS CHRISTIANITY

"You have the poor with you always, and whenever you wish you may do them good; but Me you do not have always"

T here was certainly no ambiguity amongst those who penned the Bible *(under the inspiration of the Holy Spirit)* whether one should be rich or not. The standard of living encouraged requires one to have at least *seven* streams of income.

Ship your grain across the sea; after many days you may receive a return. Invest in seven ventures, yes, in eight; you do not know what disaster may come upon the land.

- Ecclesiastes 11:1-2 NIV

Living life abundantly, without lack or insufficiency, is the gold standard for godly living. Having multiple streams of income is not just a luxury, but a necessity. Most millionaires became rich by having multiple streams of income. By setting your mind to accumulating wealth this way, you avoid the boom and bust of get rich quick schemes. This takes time, patience, planning, and of course, prayer, all the spiritual qualities one needs for successful living. **GOD WANTS YOU TO BE RICH!** Never again to be broke or in financial bondage! To achieve that aim, He has given you the power to get wealth.

"And you shall remember the Lord your God, for it is He who gives you power to get wealth, that He may establish His covenant which He swore to your fathers, as it is this day."

- Deuteronomy 8:18

God made a covenant for you to get wealth. A covenant is the most binding contract one can enter into, and breaking it has grave consequences. Therefore, you must be as serious about getting wealth as God was in empowering you to have it. Not only that, but once you have gained wealth, you must make it clear to everyone that **God made you rich!**

*"Beware that you do not forget the Lord your God by not keeping His commandments, His judgments, and His statutes which I command you today, lest **when you have eaten and are full, and have built beautiful houses and dwell in them; and when your herds and your flocks multiply, and your silver and your gold are multiplied, and all that you have is multiplied;** when your heart is lifted up, and you forget the Lord your God who brought you out of the land of Egypt, from the house of bondage; who led you through that great and terrible wilderness, in which were fiery serpents and scorpions and thirsty land where there was no water; who brought water for you out of the flinty rock; who fed you in the wilderness with manna, which your fathers did not know, that He might humble you and that He might test you, to do you good in the end then you say in your heart, **'My power and the might of my hand have gained me this wealth.'** And you shall remember the Lord your God, **for it is He who gives you power to get wealth, that He may establish His covenant which He swore to your fathers, as it is this day."***

> **You must be as serious about getting wealth as God was in empowering you to have it.**

- Deuteronomy 8:18

I will say it again; God wants everyone to know that **He made you rich!** So never feel embarrassed about being so. There are only two major mistakes you can make in regards to being rich:

1. Thinking you made yourself rich.

Both riches and honour come from You, And You reign over all. In Your hand is power and might; In Your hand it is to make great and to give strength to all. (1 Chronicles 29:12)

2. Putting your trust in your riches.

He who trusts in his riches will fall, but the righteous will flourish like the green leaf. (Proverbs 11:28 NIV)

If you are rich, and you recognize God as your provider, then you should let everybody know that it was Him, that gave you the power to get wealth.

Take note of what God stated in Deuteronomy 8:18,

"When you have eaten and are full."
"When you have built beautiful houses and dwell in them."
"When your silver and your gold has multiplied."
"When all that you have is multiplied."

GOD WANTS YOU TO THRIVE, NOT JUST SURVIVE!

Therefore, raise your standard to thriving and not just surviving. Having one house may well be enough to survive, but dwelling in beautiful houses may be what you need to thrive. Having a job may be enough to survive, but having multiple streams of income is what you need to thrive. God wants to supply your need according to *His* riches in glory, rather than by your low self-worth.

EXTRAVAGANCE

Thriving is the standard of living God desires for His children. It is His will for you to live abundantly, and have more than you need. In God's dictionary, *extravagance does not equate to waste!* Indeed, godliness, humility and extravagance go hand in hand. This may not rest well with many Christians, nevertheless, the Bible attests to that fact that God is extravagant! Extravagant in living...

He has cattle on a thousand hills *(Psalms 50:10)*

He has a house with many mansions *(John 14:2)*

The walls of His city are made of jasper and garnished with all manner of precious stones *(Revelations 21:19)*

The streets in heaven are made with gold so pure, it looks like clear glass *(Revelations 21:21)*

And in giving...

He does exceedingly and abundantly above what we ask or think. *(Ephesians 3:20)*

He pours out blessings from heaven that we cannot contain. *(Malachi 3:10)*

He satisfies us abundantly with the *fatness* of His house and causes us to drink from the river of His pleasures. *(Psalms 36:8)*

He gave King Solomon what he did not ask for – riches and honor like no other. *(1 Kings 3:13)*

That being said,

"IS IT WASTEFUL FOR A CHRISTIAN TO HAVE, FOR THEIR OWN PERSONAL USE, SOMETHING THAT IS EXTRAVAGANT OR VERY EXPENSIVE IN PRICE?"

As long as the quality matches the price tag or it is being put to good use, should it really matter? Consider Christ's response to being anointed with a fragrance oil worth more than three times the average yearly wage!

And being in Bethany at the house of Simon the leper, as He sat at the table, a woman [Mary Magdalene] came having an alabaster flask of very costly oil of spikenard. Then she broke the flask and poured it on His head. But there were some who were indignant among themselves, and said,

"Why was this fragrant oil wasted?

For it might have been sold for more than three hundred denarii and given to the poor." And they criticized her sharply. But Jesus said, "Let her alone. Why do you trouble her? She has done a good work for Me. For you have the poor with you always, and whenever you wish you may do them good; but Me you do not have always. She has done what she could. She has come beforehand to anoint My body for burial.

- Matthew 14:3-8

Spikenard is a plant that only grows in the Himalayan mountains of India and Nepal. The fragrant oil made from the plant was a rare, imported product in Israel, hence the hefty price tag. According to the disciples, the flask of spikenard oil had an estimated value of more than 300 denarii - a day's wage for a common laborer. The average day's pay for a laborer in the USA is $120. By that estimate, the value of the oil that was poured on Jesus' head is around $36,000 in today's economy.

The disciples' response to what Mary had done was one of *indignation*. Indignation is a feeling of righteous anger. It is the anger felt about something seen, done, or said that is considered morally wrong. Jesus' disciples were indignant because, from their point of view, pouring such an expensive oil on His head was considered *a waste*. They justified their anger, arguing that,

'the oil could have been sold for a great price,
and the money given to the poor.'

This sentiment has been the rallying cry against any 'believer' owning anything extravagant, such as a luxury sports car, a boat, *or even a plane*. This is the case, no matter how much they have already given to those in need.

"HOWEVER, WHAT IS REALLY BEING IMPLIED HERE?"

Putting aside the fact that it was Mary's prerogative to do what she wants with her expensive luxury item - if the oil should be sold and the proceeds given to the poor, **then someone has to buy it**. That being the case,

"IS THE BUYER MORE DESERVING OF THE EXPENSIVE LUXURY ITEM THAN CHRIST?"

"MOREOVER, IS THE BUYER MORE DESERVING OF THE EXPENSIVE LUXURY ITEM THAN YOU?"

In this present time, the expensive luxury item could be a:

- Clive Christian Sandalwood perfume ($8000)
- Hublot Swiss Watch ($43,000)
- Louis Vuitton crocodile-skin handbag ($55,500)
- Lamborghini Huracán ($300,000)
- Khalilah superyacht ($33M)
- Gulfstream G700 private jet ($75M)

Or any other high-end luxury product.

If as a Christian, you are uncomfortable with believers enjoying such luxuries, you may well feel such items should be *sold and the money given to the poor*. After-all, *that would be the Christian thing to do*. Please don't get me wrong, I whole-heartedly believe that everyone should strive to become a philanthropic giver. I applaud those who, from their abundance, have given away cars and houses to help those in need. But this should be done cheerfully, and *in love*. Not under compulsion, misplaced criticism, or by being made to feel guilty for being rich!

Jesus' response to all this, is far removed from a typical Christian response. First of all, He shuts down the woman's critics, making it clear that what she has done *is not wasteful but a good thing* and should therefore be left alone! He then goes on to say,

"You have the poor with you always,
and whenever you wish you may do them good;
but Me you do not have always."

What a statement! How would you react to any prominent Pastor, criticized over their wealth, giving the same response? [selah] At first glance, Jesus' statement seems callous and selfish, but upon quick reflection this is not the case.

The disciple's indignation at the oil being wasted, implies 2 things:

1. **Jesus is not worthy to be anointed with so expensive an oil.**
2. **A perception that there is lack and insufficiency.**

In contrast, Jesus' response stems from the fact that:

1. **He is worth infinitely more than any item of great price.**
In addition, *you too* are infinitely more valuable than any expensive luxury item, having been made in the image of God. As such, expensive luxury items are for your enjoyment when it is in your means to do so.

2. **In the Kingdom of Heaven, there is no such thing as lack and insufficiency.** A believer can make a *withdrawal* whenever they wish for the benefit of those in need, as well as for themselves.

Jesus demonstrated the Kingdom when He fed more than 5000 people from just five loaves and two fish *(Matthew 14:15-21)*. He did the same when He fed more than 4000 people from just seven loaves and a few fish *(Matthew 15:32-39)*. Both of these events happened in remote and deserted places. These are just two of the many *'works'*

> **Godliness, humility and extravagance go hand in hand.**

He did to demonstrate the Kingdom. His entire ministry on earth was spent demonstrating the fact that:

'There is a spiritual dimension of unlimited resources and power available to all who would believe. This is the Kingdom of God, which is in you. It's power and resources can be manifested in your life, and in the lives of others, through the faith of the Son of God.'

This is the gospel of the Kingdom. The gospel that Jesus preached! This is the gospel the disciples witnessed *'up close and personal'* in the three years they spent under Jesus' tutelage. Not only did they witness the feeding of the multitudes, but they were also the ones handing out the food!

They were there when Jesus turned water into wine.
(John 2:1-11)

They were there when a colossal haul of fish was caught. This was done, at Jesus' command, after they had spent the whole night fishing without any success. *(Luke 5:1-11)*

They were there when Jesus commanded Peter to go to the lake, open the mouth of the first fish he caught, take the coins he will find in there, and pay the temple tax for them both. *(Matthew 17:27)*

And...

They all knew that Jesus was the Christ, the Son of the living God. *(Matthew 16:16)*

Given all that they knew and witnessed firsthand,

"WHY WOULD THEY CONSIDER THE POURING OF OIL ON JESUS' HEAD TO BE A WASTE AND MORALLY WRONG?"

Also…

"WHY WOULD THEY EVEN SUGGEST SELLING THE OIL TO FEED THE POOR, HAVING WITNESSED THE UNLIMITED POWER AND RESOURCES OF THE KINGDOM?"

No matter how expensive the oil was, this line of thinking not only contradicts the gospel of the Kingdom, but is also an *insult* to Christ! Anyone who criticizes and insults any believer because of their wealth is also criticizing and insulting 'The One' through whom such wealth came. To be in Christ, is to be *'at one'* with God. What belongs to Him, belongs to you.

That being said, I do not believe the disciples would knowingly insult Christ in the way they did. As a matter-of-fact, I don't believe any Christian would knowingly insult Christ, as they do, when they criticize their fellow brothers and sisters for being *too* wealthy! Given what the disciples knew about Christ, it is surprising they felt so indignant about what the woman did with the oil.

"SO, WHERE DID THE NOTION OF THE OIL BEING WASTED REALLY COME FROM?"

The answer can be found when you read John's account of this event:

*Then Mary took a pound of very costly oil of spikenard, anointed the feet of Jesus, and wiped His feet with her hair. And the house was filled with the fragrance of the oil. Then one of His disciples, **Judas Iscariot**, Simon's son, who would betray Him, said,*

"Why was this fragrant oil not sold for three hundred denarii and given to the poor?"

*This he said, not that he cared for the poor, but because **he was a thief**, and had the money box; and he used to take what was put in it.*

- John 12:3-6

Judas was the instigator and catalyst for the disciple's misplaced indignation! He was the one who implied that the expensive oil was being wasted on Jesus when he said, *"Why was this fragrant oil not sold for three hundred denarii and given to the poor?"* Due to his trusted position as the treasurer *(keeper of the money box)*, his opinion carried a lot of weight; causing the rest of the disciples to fall into his line of thinking. However, whilst the disciple's reaction stemmed from a moral standpoint, Judas' comments stemmed from an immoral motive. Judas was a thief! He regularly syphoned money from the money box, which must have contained a considerable amount, as none of the other disciples noticed anything missing. Worse still is the fact that he was under the direct influence of Satan. We know this because on the eve of Christ's betrayal, the Bible informs us that Satan *entered* Judas.

*Now the Feast of Unleavened Bread drew near, which is called Passover. And the chief priests and the scribes sought how they might kill Him, for they feared the people. **Then Satan entered Judas, surnamed Iscariot,** who was numbered among the twelve. So he went his way and conferred with the chief priests and captains, how he might betray Him to them.*

- Luke 22:1-4

Although Judas was the ringleader, Satan was the one pulling the strings! He obviously had Judas under his deceptive sway for some time, to the point that he could walk right into him when the opportunity came. This reflects how open Judas was to Satan's way of thinking. Satan is the father of lies, and the accuser of the brethren. The accusation levelled against Mary, bares the blueprint for all his schemes:

An ungodly agenda - cloaked in morality - executed through blind zeal and righteous indignation.

DON'T BE DECEIVED

We must, therefore, be aware of the perniciousness of Satan, who is well versed in polluting minds and infecting paradigms. He does this by sowing the seeds of his thoughts, into the collective conscious of the masses. Even the church! His method of deception will always involve:

• Exploiting your ignorance of God's word
• Exploiting your ignorance of your divine identity.

This is the strategy he used on Eve, in tempting her to eat the forbidden fruit.

Now the serpent was more cunning than any beast of the field which the Lord God had made. And he said to the woman, "Has God indeed said, 'You shall not eat of every tree of the garden?'" And the woman said to the serpent,

"We may eat the fruit of the trees of the garden; but of the fruit of the tree which is in the midst of the garden, God has said, 'You shall not eat it, nor shall you touch it, lest you die.'

"Then the serpent said to the woman, "You will not surely die. For God knows that in the day you eat of it your eyes will be opened, and you will be like God, knowing good and evil."

- Genesis 3:1-5

First of all, God did not say they will die if they *touched* the fruit! He only said they will die if they *eat* the fruit. As Adam was the one God gave this command to, he may have been the one who *added* this extra stipulation as a preventative measure for Eve. Nevertheless, it was a deviation that could easily be exploited. Imagine what went through Eve's mind when she reached out and touched the fruit and *did not die*. Straight away it would seem that the serpent was telling the truth! This then made it easier for her to proceed with disobeying God's command.

Secondly, Eve was tempted by the suggestion that she could be like God if she ate the fruit.' However, as she was already like God, having been made in His image, it would seem she was deceived into eating the fruit due to her ignorance of her divine identity.

It only takes a slight deviation from God's word to bring us into bondage, whether that be in our relationships, health, career, or finances, This, coupled with ignorance of our true identity, has brought untold devastation to the world, impacting all of our lives in one way or another. As the title of this chapter implies, there is a disparity between Christ and many aspects of Christianity brought about by a deviation from the word of God and ignorance of our divine identity. This is not said to offend anyone but to bring awareness of where many Christians are in relation to Christ.

A key area of this disparity lies in how Jesus is perceived. This is of grave importance because the most important tenet of the Christian faith, is for believers to be *like* Christ, having been *conformed* to His image.

For whom He foreknew, He also predestined to be conformed to the image of His Son, that He might be the firstborn among many brethren.

- Romans 8:29

To be conformed to the image of Christ is to embrace the thinking, character, and *self-image* of Christ. You cannot conform to the image of the Son with the wrong perception of Him. No more so is the image of Christ impaired than the perception of Him being *poor!* Many Christians' attitudes towards wealth, spirituality, identity, and life as a whole stem from the perception of Christ being poor! However, not only does this misconception impact the church but the world as a whole. Christian values stemming from how Christ is perceived influence us all in varying degrees. Most of these values serve to progress society and humanity at large. However, there is a Christian value, insidious in nature, that has adversely affected and infected many cultures and societies, that being the so-called 'Virtue of poverty.'

Throughout the centuries, the virtue of poverty has had the knock-on effect of impeding the finances, ambitions, potential, and even the health of millions of unsuspecting well-intentioned individuals caught up in its long-reaching tentacles. Although only a relatively small number of people take a vow of poverty, the idea of poverty being virtuous (implying that to be rich is ungodly) has negatively impacted the thinking, education, and decision-making of billions of hard-working people across the globe.

A not too distant relative of the virtue of poverty is the belief that one should not strive to be rich but *comfortable*. Although being comfortable means different things to different people, it generally means being able to:

• Pay for your all bills and living expenses
• Pay off any debt (or keep up on loans and credit card payments)
• Drive a new car
• Go on holidays
• Put money away for a rainy day
• Help out friends and family members
• Improve the overall quality of your life.

Although on the surface this may seem quite reasonable, it is one of the most selfish ambitions one could have. Especially if you are a Christian! This is certainly not the thinking of our heavenly Father, who desires to:

- Pour out for you such blessing that there
  will not be room enough to receive it,
- Lavishly satisfy you with the fullness of His house
  and cause you to drink from the rivers of His pleasures,
- Do exceedingly and abundantly above all that you ask or think,

And so much more.

All for the purpose of you being a blessing to your community, and to the nations. We all have a responsibility to *'be more'* so that we can *'have more'* and *'do more'* to improve the lives of others. God's model for living is for our *'cup to run over,'* so that from the overflow of abundance, we can make a significant difference in the world.

CHAPTER 3

PROFILE OF GOD'S LEADING SERVANTS

---◆---

*"Let the LORD be magnified, who has pleasure
in the prosperity of His servant"*

G od takes pleasure in the prosperity of His servant, and we certainly see evidence of this throughout the Bible. If you look at the lives of the most prolific of God's servants, you will find they were no stranger to wealth and riches. As a matter of fact, they were super-rich!

ABRAHAM'S WEALTH

Abraham's wealth is the very first context in which 'wealth' is mentioned in the Bible. Genesis 13 informs us that he was rich in livestock as well as in silver and gold. He also had his own personal army! His nephew, Lot, who traveled with him, was also rich in livestock, and their combined possessions were so great that the land could not support them being together!

ISAAC'S WEALTH

Abraham's son, Isaac, lived in the land of the Philistines and was a very prosperous man. Genesis 26 tells us that he became rich and prospered more and more, until he became very wealthy! So much so that the Philistines envied him. In the end, Abimelech, King of the Philistines, told him to depart from the land because he had become too powerful.

JACOB'S WEALTH

Although Jacob was a trickster by name and by deed, he was an exceedingly blessed man. He was extraordinarily skilled in raising sheep and cattle. So much so that his father-in-law, Laban, became very wealthy just by having him in his service. When the time came for him to branch out from under Laban with his growing family, the Bible says he increased exceedingly, and had much cattle, and maidservants, and menservants, and camels, and asses *(Genesis 30:43)*.

JOB'S WEALTH

Apart from Jesus, Job was one of two men in the Bible, described as blameless or perfect in their walk with God. He was also, in his time, the greatest man of all the people in the East – possessing seven thousand sheep, three thousand camels, five hundred yokes of oxen, five hundred female donkeys, and an enormous household. By conservative estimation, Job's net worth in livestock before the tribulation he endured would amount to over $28M in today's economy. However, after his tribulation, having lost all but his wife, the Lord *'blessed his latter days more than his beginning'* with twice the number of livestock he had before, increasing his net worth to around $56M in today's economy.

JOSEPH'S WEALTH

Although Joseph was born into a wealthy family, his is a story of rags to riches, having been sold into slavery by his own brothers. However, even as a slave, the Bible describes him as a *'prosperous man'* because **the Lord was with him** *(Genesis 39:2)*. He also had the divine gift of interpreting dreams, and this spiritual gift became key to his rise to prominence.

Despite being falsely accused of attempted rape and thrown into prison, his gift eventually brought him before the King of Egypt. When he interpreted the King's dream, he became the second most powerful man in what was, at the time, the wealthiest and most advanced nation in the known world.

ELISHA'S WEALTH

Elisha was the protegee and successor of Elijah the prophet. Although next to nothing is known about his life before meeting Elijah, the number of oxen he was ploughing with when he encountered Elijah, indicates he was from a wealthy land-owning family *(1 Kings 19:19)*. He is without a doubt, one of the most prolific of the old testament prophets, having inherited a double portion of Elijah's spirit. However, unlike his former master, who was a very solitary figure, Elisha was often found in the company of the kings of Israel. He was also a house owner, even though his ministry took him far and wide. Although, he refused *'the blessing'* offered by Naaman, consisting of:

- 10 talents of silver,
- 6000 pieces of gold,
- 10 changes of raiment
  (which in today's economy would have run into millions of dollars),

there's no indication he refused the King of Syria's gift of 60 camels laden with *'every good thing of Damascus.'* The camels alone would be worth close to a million dollars in today's economy, and in keeping with ancient customs, the gifts they carried would amount to many millions more!

DANIEL'S WEALTH

Daniel's story is very much like Joseph's. He, too, was born into wealth and nobility but taken into slavery *(in Babylon)*. Like Joseph, he had the divine gift of interpreting dreams, which was instrumental to his rise to prominence. When he interpreted the King Nebuchadnezzar's dream, *(a dream that could not be interpreted by the wisemen of Babylon)* he was lavished with many *'great gifts.'* Hopefully, by now, you've realized that in the ancient world, a 'gift' from a King, or someone of great influence, usually amounts to several million dollars in today's economy. Daniel was also made ruler over the whole province of Babylon and chief of the governors over all the wise men of Babylon *(Daniel 2:48).*

So, being rich and wealthy was pretty much the status quo for God's leading servants. They most likely would have been ranked amongst the super-rich elite of this present time. Be this as it may, their wealth and riches amounted to 'pocket-change,' compared to the personal fortunes and vast revenues of the Kings of Israel. In particular, David and Solomon.

DAVID'S WEALTH

King David's wealth was such, that near the end of his life, he bequeathed to his son, Solomon what was needed to construct the temple.

Indeed, I have taken much trouble to prepare for the house of the Lord one hundred thousand talents of gold and one million talents of silver, and bronze and iron beyond measure, for it is so abundant. I have prepared timber and stone also, and you may add to them.

- 1 Chronicles 22:14

The standard weight used for trading gold and silver in today's economy is the troy ounce. 100,000 talents of gold converts to around 96,452239.71 troy ounces. Given that gold is currently trading at around $1,550 per troy ounce (January 2020), David's donation of gold amounts to over $149.5 Billion. His donation of silver (based on the current price of $18 per troy ounce) amounts to over $17.3 Billion. Let's not forget the bronze and iron that was too innumerable to measure! This donation to the building of God's temple was by no means the totality of David's wealth. Much of his fortune came from the spoils of his many military victories. He also received a tribute from the Moabites and probably other nations around him.

SOLOMON'S WEALTH

Although, King Solomon inherited his father's wealth, God still took it upon Himself to bless him with far more wealth. More than any other King before or after him!

Solomon went up there to the bronze altar before the Lord, which was at the tabernacle of meeting, and offered a thousand burnt offerings on it. On that night, God appeared to Solomon, and said to him, "Ask! What shall I give you?" And Solomon said to God: "You have shown great mercy to David my father, and have made me king in his place. Now, O Lord God, let Your promise to David my father be established, for You have made me king over a people like the dust of the earth in multitude. Now give me wisdom and knowledge, that I may go out and come in before this people; for who can judge this great people of Yours?"

And God said to Solomon: "Because this was in your heart, and you have not asked riches or wealth or honour or the life of your enemies, nor have you asked long life - but have asked wisdom and knowledge for yourself, that you may judge My people over whom I have made you king - wisdom and knowledge are granted to you; and I will give you riches and wealth and honour, such as none of the kings have had who were before you, nor shall any after you have the like."

- 2 Chronicles 1:6-12

Much of this wealth was manifested in the form of gifts from the many dignitaries and heads of state that travelled from all around the world to seek Solomon's wisdom. One such person was the Queen of Sheba, who was so impressed with Solomon's wisdom and opulence, that she gave him, *'one hundred and twenty talents of gold, spices in great abundance, and precious stones' (2 Chronicles 9:9)*. The gold alone equates to $179.4 Million in today's economy. Other revenues came, thanks to his large shipping fleet and his partnership with the King of Tyre. Through this partnership, he acquired $628 Million worth of gold overseas, as well as many other exotic goods.

Apart from what was brought to him by merchants and Arabian Kings, he also received an annual tribute of six hundred and sixty-six talents of gold from the Kingdoms he ruled over. That equates to just under $996 Million in annual tributes alone.

To reiterate, wealth and riches were the status quo of God's leading servants, as well as those who walked in His ways. However, in the biblical narrative, not one of these great men of God are known for or defined by their wealth.

- Abraham is known for being 'the father of faith.'

- Isaac represents 'God's promise' the miracle child born, as a result of 'hope against hope.'

- Jacob, who became Israel, was known as the one who has 'struggled with God and with men and prevailed.'

These three patriarchs had the privilege of their names mentioned whenever God introduces Himself as - The God of Abraham, Isaac, and Jacob.

- Elisha is known for being the revolutionary prophet who had a double portion of Elijah's spirit.

- Job is known for his unshakeable faith in God, despite the numerous afflictions set upon him.

- Joseph and Daniel, are known for being the great interpreters of visions and dreams.

- Daniel was also known for his outstanding faith when thrown in the lion den under the penalty of death.

- David is known for being the 'worshipping warrior.' The only man to be described as 'being after God's own heart.'

- Solomon is known for being the wisest man that ever lived.

All were fabulously rich! But their righteousness and acts of faith, far outshone the riches they possessed. More importantly, their wealth did not get in the way of their relationship with God. As a matter-of-fact, their wealth emanated *from* their relationship with God, as He poured out His goodness and blessing in their lives. These blessings came in the form of 'divine gifts and power' that made many of them valuable assets to their nation.

CHAPTER 4

THE GRACE OF OUR LORD JESUS

---◆---

"For you know the grace of our Lord Jesus Christ, that though He was rich, yet for your sakes He became poor"

C harles Spurgeon's assertion that it is *'Anti-Christian and unholy for any Christian to live with the object of accumulating wealth'* was part of a sermon he preached in 1867, entitled: 'Our Lord's Involuntary Poverty.' The thinking behind this sermon is based on how the following scripture is often interpreted:

For you know the grace of our Lord Jesus Christ, that though He was rich, yet for your sakes He became poor, that you through His poverty might become rich.

- 2 Corinthians 8:9

It is widely believed that the above text is *clear proof* that Christ was only rich in His *preincarnate*, heavenly existence. But, for our sakes, He relinquished His *'heavenly riches'* to live a life of poverty, having been born to an impoverished carpenter and his wife. Charles Spurgeon goes onto say,

"There was no period of the Savior's life on earth in which it could be said that He was rich, but He became poor. It must, therefore, have been in a previous state of being that our Lord was rich—and I shall now ask your thoughts to go back to the time when Jesus Christ was rich. Poor are our words!"

That being the case, we should *follow Jesus' example* and seek only to be rich *spiritually* while being materially poor. According to Spurgeon, those who follow the example of Christ in this way are considered to be *'Advanced Christians.'* He goes on to applaud the likes of John Wesley, who died in poverty leaving but *'two spoons,'* having served God with all that he had.

I whole-heartedly agree that we should follow Jesus' example. As a-matter-of-fact it is imperative that we do! However, as I will show you later in this book, the widely held belief that Jesus was poor in this life, is **TOTALLY UNTRUE.**

When we consider the fact that:

1. **Poverty is a curse** *(Genesis 3:17-19)*
2. **Christ only became a curse on the cross** *(Galatians 3:13)*
3. **Therefore, any exchange from being rich to becoming poor could only have took place on the cross** *(2 Corinthians 5:21)*

...then the Apostle Paul's statement regarding *'the grace of our Lord Jesus Christ,'* is *clear proof* that Jesus was indeed rich in this life, and not just in heaven! Therefore, the example we must follow is:

'Being rich like Jesus'

We must follow the Lord's example of having immense wealth but not allowing that wealth to have mastery over our lives.

Even if we entertained the notion that Christ was only rich in heaven, and we should, therefore, follow His example as a poor person in this world, how do you reconcile that belief with the fact that *"As He is, so are we in this world." (1 John 4:17).* The Bible says, **"As He is,"** (present tense) not, **'As He was.'** Jesus is in heaven, where, by the world's standard, He is undisputedly and unequivocally, rich beyond imagination. That being the case, no matter which side of the fence you reside, the example we must follow is:

'Being rich like Jesus'

That is the grace of our Lord Jesus. The reason He became poor *on the cross.*

CHAPTER 5

CONFRONTING THE VIRTUES OF POVERTY

"It is more blessed to give than to receive"

Although God's leading servants were all rich, it is widely perceived that it is more *'godly'* to be poor than rich. To many, wealth and riches are deemed an *'offense to faith,'* and rich people are seen as *'especially sinful.'* This belief is held despite numerous examples in the Bible of God blessing His children with material wealth. From generation to generation, Christians and non-Christians alike have been indoctrinated with this negative attitude towards being rich. However, God has put *eternity* in the hearts of us all *(Ecclesiastes 3:11)*. Therefore, we are *unlimited* by nature, equipped with an instinctive urge to *'be more,' 'do more,' 'have more,'* and *'give more.'* A poverty mindset subdues and limits what you can achieve, leaving you to live a life of untapped potential, falling short of being all that God created you to be.

Many of the perceived virtues of poverty were formed by a distorted and out-of-context interpretation of Christ's teachings. Such as not serving *'God and mammon'* – which I addressed in the first chapter. Or using Jesus' instruction to the rich young ruler to *'Sell all he had and follow Him,'* as a doctrine requiring all Christians to rid themselves of 'earthly goods' – which I will address later in this book. However, being broke or poor does not make you closer to Christ than being rich. On the contrary, 'lack' can be more distracting than material wealth, especially if your mind is preoccupied with the worry of meeting your day-to-day needs.

Being wealthy no more equates to being materialistic than being poor equates to godliness. As repeatedly demonstrated by the faith heroes of the Bible, a life of faith is determined by your relationship with God, which can be enjoyed whether one is rich or poor.

Nevertheless, many god-fearing and devout men and women, believe it is their religious duty to relinquish all their worldly possessions in order to dedicate their lives to God and help the poor. As well-intentioned it may be to take the vow of poverty to help the poor,

"IS THIS REALLY THE MOST EFFECTIVE WAY TO HELP THE POOR, OR INDEED, HUMANITY AS A WHOLE?"

Here are some reasons why this question must be asked:

WE ARE CALLED TO BE AGENTS OF CHANGE

The gospel of the Kingdom is supposed to be *'good news'* to the poor. The best news a poor person can receive is that *'they no longer need be poor.'* However, the overall aim of religious folk, who feel it necessary to be poor in order to help the poor is to bring *comfort* to the poor, or in some cases champion the cause of the poor. But where is the drive to change one's circumstances so that they are no longer poor? Indeed, how effective can you be in transforming the lives of the poor when your beliefs hinge on the virtues of poverty? You certainly will do nothing to change a person's life from poverty to prosperity! The very thing God wants above everything else *(3 John 1:2)*.

If there is a vow to be made, it should be to be an ***agent of change***, transforming lives from the grip of darkness into God's marvelous light. Darkness and light are contrasting concepts, whether that be good or evil, foolish or wise, sickness or health, rich or poor. When we allow God to use us to impact someone's life, the contrast between their past and their present circumstances should be like night and day!

WE ARE CALLED TO DO MORE GOOD

In his book, 'Business Secrets from The Bible,' Rabbi Daniel Lapin, known widely as 'America's Rabbi,' makes a startling comparison between the venerable and beatified Mother Teresa and MicroSoft founder, Bill Gates. He asks the question, **"Who out of the two did 'more good' for more people?"** This question is asked on the premise that, **'He who helps more people is doing more good than he who only helps a few.'** That being the case, although Mother Teresa is well-deserving of praise for her tireless work in caring for thousands or even hundreds of thousands of poor people in Calcutta, we should not overlook the fact that Microsoft products have improved the lives of hundreds of millions of people worldwide.

Therefore, as hard as it may be for some to hear, Bill Gates *(amongst others Billionaires)* has done more good for mankind than Mother Teresa - and this can be measured quantitively.

Here is another notable point Rabbi Lapin makes:

'Wealth is God's way of incentivizing you to do exactly what He wants you to do, which is to care obsessively about satisfying the needs and desires of His other children.' Cynics may denounce 'monetary motivation' as greed but this is false thinking.

'The virtue of service is in no way compromised or diminished by the monetary reward for doing so.'

– Rabbi Daniel Lapin

So few religious people sing Bill Gates' praises alongside Mother Teresa because they have adopted the mistaken view that *benefitting* from the good one does somehow *diminishes* the virtue of their good deeds. However, this is a 'Win-Win' because doing good for others and earning a living from it is a self-perpetuating model of success for all.

WE ARE CALLED TO BE GIVERS

If there is a virtue to be found in being poor, it is when scarcity places a greater demand for wealth to flow into your life. The saying, *"Necessity is the mother of invention,"* is not said without merit, and to quote American businessman and philanthropist, Jon Huntsman Sr,

"When facing severe challenges your mind is normally at its sharpest."

George Müller was a Prussian Christian Evangelist, who lived in Bristol, England during the 19th Century. Through prayer alone, this great man of faith built an impressive array of orphan houses that housed over 2,000 children at a time. Müller did this with no personal wealth of his own. He wanted to rescue orphans who would otherwise go to work in dangerous workhouses or live on the streets. He had a great desire to provide them with care, education and training. But his supreme motivation was the desire to give visible proof of a living God who answers prayer. To this end, he received around £1.4M in donations *(£100M in todays' economy)* during his lifetime, without asking anybody but God for a single penny.

Stories abound of God's divine provision. One breakfast time there was no food. Müller confidently said grace. Immediately there was a knock at the door. It was the local baker who had woken in the night with a feeling that God was telling him the orphans had no bread. So at 2.00am, he got up and baked some for them. Shortly after this came another knock at the door, the milkman's wagon had broken down outside the orphanage. He asked if he could give them his milk, so as to be able to empty and repair his wagon. There was also another time when a young woman from a very wealthy family donated almost three quarters of a million dollars in jewels.

In addition to George Müller's faith, what should be duly noted is the role of those whom God used to fulfill what was asked for in prayer. As Müller made it a policy never to ask anyone for money, the gifts and large sums of money that was donated to his ministry could only have been done by *God's hand* on the lives of those who were well able to give.

Often times, God uses wealthy people who are compassionate and giving, to answer the prayers of the poor in need. Take for example the good Samaritan who found a man robbed, beaten, and left for dead by the wayside. Not only did he have the compassion to stop and tend to his wounds, he also took him to an inn and paid the inn-keeper two denarii *(two days wages for a common laborer)* to take care of the man in his absence. He also promised to repay the inn-keeper whatever more was spent upon his return. The fact that he could make such a promise could only mean that the good Samaritan was rich.

Therefore, it is wrong to joyfully receive donations from wealthy people in one hand, and then tear them down for being rich with the other.

You will do well to remember that being able to give substantially to those in need is a key role of a believer. It is to a believer's credit to lend to others *without expecting anything back*. This can hardly be done by those who choose to live a life of poverty!

*If you lend to those from whom you hope to receive back, what credit is that to you? For even sinners lend to sinners to receive as much back. But love your enemies, do good, **and lend, hoping for nothing in return;** and your reward will be great, and you will be sons of the Most High.*

- Luke 6:34-35

THE WEALTH OF THE EARLY BELIEVERS

Finally, I would like to address the fact that the vow of poverty taken by various religious orders is the furthest thing from poverty, as they do not live the life of destitution you may think they do! Take for example the St. Augustinians, a Christian order founded in 1244. Under what they label as *communal poverty*, everything is shared and no individual calls anything their own. The devotees live together in comfortable homes with heating and air conditioning. They eat well, dress comfortably, and drive well maintained cars. Any money received by any one individual is placed in a community bank account and subsequently gets used for the needs of the members and the work of the ministry. This is supposed to be modelled after the early Christian communities described in the book of Acts:

Now the multitude of those who believed were of one heart and one soul; neither did anyone say that any of the things he possessed was his own, but they had all things in common. And with great power the apostles gave witness to the resurrection of the Lord Jesus. And great grace was upon them all. **Nor was there anyone among them who lacked; for all who were possessors of lands or houses sold them, and brought the proceeds of the things that were sold, and laid them at the apostles' feet; and they distributed to each as anyone had need.**

- Acts 4:32-35

Although on the surface, it appears that the early believers lived void of any possessions, **this was not the case.** They were so united in their hearts that no one individual considered what they possessed as their own. In a show of solidarity *(which was needful at the time due to how they were persecuted and ostracized)* all who were possessors of lands or houses sold them. It is important to note, that the believers that had land and property to sell for such a purpose could only have been the wealthy landowners who converted to Christ. It is also important to note that they did not sell the homes they lived in! For it was in *their homes* that the community of believers were able to break bread, fellowship and praise God (Acts 2:46). This they did out of love and a common goal. It was not done as a *requirement* for becoming a believer.

To further clarify this position, let us look at the case of Ananias and Sapphira, who's sudden death for withholding part of the proceeds of the land they sold, struck fear in the hearts of those who heard about it.

But a certain man named Ananias, with Sapphira his wife, sold a possession. And he kept back part of the proceeds, his wife also being aware of it, and brought a certain part and laid it at the apostles' feet. But Peter said, "Ananias, why has Satan filled your heart to lie to the Holy Spirit and keep back part of the price of the land for yourself? **While it remained, was it not your own? And after it was sold, was it not in your own control?** *Why have you conceived this thing in your heart? You have not lied to men but to God." Then Ananias, hearing these words, fell down and breathed his last. So great fear came upon all those who heard these things. And the young men arose and wrapped him up, carried him out, and buried him.*

Now it was about three hours later when his wife came in, not knowing what had happened. And Peter answered her, "Tell me whether you sold the land for so much?" She said, "Yes, for so much." Then Peter said to her, "How is it that you have agreed together to test the Spirit of the Lord? Look, the feet of those who have buried your husband are at the door, and they will carry you out." Then immediately she fell down at his feet and breathed her last. And the young men came in and found her dead, and carrying her out, buried her by her husband. So great fear came upon all the church and upon all who heard these things.

- Acts 5: 1-11

Ananias and Sapphira sold a piece of land they possessed *(not their home)* but withheld some of the proceeds from the sale. The questions is,

WERE THEY REQUIRED TO GIVE ALL THE PROCEEDS OF THE PIECE OF LAND THEY SOLD?

Not at all! In his condemnation, Peter said it was *their choice* whether to sell the land or not, and after they sold it, it was *their choice* as to how much of the proceeds they wanted to give.

IN THAT CASE, WHY DID THEY DIE?

They died because they wanted to make out that they were giving all of the proceeds of the land they sold. The only reason for this is because they wanted to *appear* righteous. Like the Pharisees, and the Sadducees, they were only interested in the outward appearance of righteousness, rather than having a clean heart. They were what Jesus described as, *"Whitewashed tombs which indeed appear beautiful outwardly, but inside are full of dead men's bones and all uncleanness."* (Matthew 23:27)

Self-induced poverty was not the motivation or requirement for the believers of the early church. What they practiced was not communal poverty but *communal wealth.* Many of them were exchanging *personal* wealth for **shared wealth.** They did this so that **none who was amongst them would be in lack or need.** Poverty, therefore, was not what the early believers were trying to promote. It was what they were trying to ELIMINATE!

• Poverty is not a virtue.
• Poverty is a curse.
• Poverty is not godly.
• God wants poverty eliminated.

The communal wealth model was the most practical means for the early believers to eliminate any lack or need from amongst them. The type of need that could only be met financially. As exemplified by the Augustinians, any group or religious order modelling the lifestyle of the early believers, will inevitably be *'better off'* than those who are poor or struggling to pay their own bills.

Don't be duped into thinking that living without any earthly goods is the godly way to live. It is doubtful that the early believers would have sold their lands and properties if no one amongst them were in lack or need!

It is not the will of God for you to be in lack in any area of your life. That is why He made it a promise to personally meet all your needs.

My God shall supply all your need according to
His riches in glory by Christ Jesus.
- Philippians 4:19 -

CHAPTER 6

BORN INTO WEALTH

———————◆———————

She wrapped Him in swaddling clothes, and laid Him in a manger,
because there was no room for them in the inn...

I t is often taught by teachers and scholars alike that Joseph and Mary were poor. There is also a claim that in his occupation as a carpenter, Joseph would have been among the poorest of the poor. Too poor to own farmland, uneducated, and forced to live off whatever carpentry or laboring work he could find.

Further *perceived* evidence of their poverty can be found when Mary and Joseph took Jesus to the temple in Jerusalem to be dedicated to the Lord.

And when eight days were completed for the circumcision of the Child, His name was called Jesus, the name given by the angel before He was conceived in the womb. Now when the days of her purification according to the law of Moses were completed, they brought Him to Jerusalem to present Him to the Lord (as it is written in the law of the Lord, "Every male who opens the womb shall be called holy to the Lord"), and to offer a sacrifice according to what is said in the law of the Lord, "A pair of turtledoves or two young pigeons."

- Luke 2:21-24

The requirement for the firstborn male to be presented to the Lord in such a manner can be found in the book of Leviticus, where many such rituals and sacrifices are detailed. In all but the King James Version of the Bible, the offering of a pair of turtledoves or two young pigeons is interpreted as a provision Moses made for those who *could not* afford to bring what was really required - that being a lamb. Therefore, a pair of turtledoves or two young pigeons is deemed as the *poor person's sacrifice.*

" 'When the days of her purification for a son or daughter are over, she is to bring to the priest at the entrance to the tent of meeting a year-old lamb for a burnt offering and a young pigeon or a dove for a sin offering. He shall offer them before the LORD to make atonement for her, and then she will be ceremonially clean from her flow of blood. " 'These are the regulations for the woman who

gives birth to a boy or a girl. But if she cannot afford a lamb, she is to bring two doves or two young pigeons, one for a burnt offering and the other for a sin offering. In this way the priest will make atonement for her, and she will be clean.' "

- Leviticus 12:6-8 (NIV)

Although this all seems like *evidence* of Joseph and Mary's poverty, further study will reveal that this is not the case.

Let us first address the claim that as a carpenter, Joseph would have been classed amongst the poorest of the poor. To address this claim, we must delve into the social structure of Judaean society.

THE HAVE'S AND THE HAVE NOTS

To date, the only source of information on Judaean society in ancient times is the Bible. Archaeological excavations have so far produced no significant additional material on this subject; nor have the few epigraphical sources discovered in Palestine, added to our knowledge in this field. The grassroots aspects of society and social problems were of incidental interest to the writers. Therefore, it is only *indirectly* that the Bible permits us to view the social structure and customs of this ancient era. So here is what we have been able to glean:

There was a considerable gap between the rich and the poor, with probably a very slim middle-class. We, therefore, have a society primarily comprised of 'The Haves' and 'The Have Nots.' 'The Haves' *owned* the land, and 'The Have Nots' *worked* the land. There are many examples of wealthy landowners in the Bible, such as Abraham,

Isaac, and Jacob. Wealthy landowners are also featured in some of Jesus' parables.

Those who worked the land are also mentioned in Jesus' parables, such as sowers, farmers, and hired hands. Those who were extremely poor were badly treated in Judaean society and seen as social outcasts. This ostracism was largely based on the doctrine of 'reward and punishment' where adherence to God's commandments brings prosperity and well-being and disobedience, poverty, and destruction. However, James gives a sharp rebuke against such hostility towards the poor, especially when it takes place within the church:

My brethren, do not hold the faith of our Lord Jesus Christ, the Lord of glory, with partiality. For if there should come into your assembly a man with gold rings, in fine apparel, and there should also come in a poor man in filthy clothes, and you pay attention to the one wearing the fine clothes and say to him, "You sit here in a good place," and say to the poor man, "You stand there," or, "Sit here at my footstool," have you not shown partiality among yourselves, and become judges with evil thoughts?

- James 2:1-4

Alongside the wealthy landowning class were merchants, royal functionaries, religious leaders, government officials, elite fishing families, and *artisans*. Artisans were an essential class of skilled craftsmen such as engravers, embroiders, goldsmiths, stonecutters, and of course, *carpenters*. Most of the Pharisees came from middle-class artisans, such as the apostle Paul who was a tentmaker. In addition, artisans played a vital role in spiritual life, as they were relied upon for the critical task of building the tabernacle, the temple, and the ark of the covenant.

Then the Lord spoke to Moses, saying:

"See, I have called by name Bezalel the son of Uri, the son of Hur, of the tribe of Judah. And I have filled him with the Spirit of God, in wisdom, in understanding, in knowledge, and in all manner of workmanship, to design artistic works, to work in gold, in silver, in bronze, in cutting jewels for setting, in carving wood, and to work in all manner of workmanship.

And I, indeed I, have appointed with him Aholiab the son of Ahisamach, of the tribe of Dan; and I have put wisdom in the hearts of all who are gifted artisans, that they may make all that I have commanded you: the tabernacle of meeting, the ark of the Testimony and the mercy seat that is on it, and all the furniture of the tabernacle - the table and its utensils, the pure gold lampstand with all its utensils, the altar of incense, the altar of burnt offering with all its utensils, and the laver and its base - the garments of ministry, the holy garments for Aaron the priest and the garments of his sons, to minister as priests, and the anointing oil and sweet incense for the holy place. According to all that I have commanded you they shall do."

- Exodus 31:1-11

As a carpenter, Joseph was in *high demand* for his services, and as a result, he was a man of means. Which makes perfect sense because, in a world whose infrastructure was primarily made of wood, how could he not be!! Carpenters of ancient times were heavily involved in building ships, chariots, cities, and palaces with all the furniture and fixtures they contained.

Therefore, the notion of Joseph being amongst the poorest of the poor and having to survive hand-to-mouth by whatever carpentry work he could get is ridiculous at best!

ONLY THE RICH PAID TAXES

Further evidence of Joseph's wealth is embedded in the story behind Jesus' birth. First of all, as a descendant of David, Joseph was required to travel from Nazareth to his ancestral home, Bethlehem *(where David was born)*, to register for the tax census.

And it came to pass in those days that a decree went out from Caesar Augustus that all the world should be registered. This census first took place while Quirinius was governing Syria. So all went to be registered, everyone to his own city. Joseph also went up from Galilee, out of the city of Nazareth, into Judea, to the city of David, which is called Bethlehem, because he was of the house and lineage of David, to be registered with Mary, his betrothed wife, who was with child.

- Luke 2:1-5

This required him to enter into the public records his name, income, and any *property* he owned. If, indeed, Joseph and Mary were the poorest of the poor, with no real income or land, why would they have to register for tax? Only those who had a substantial income and property need register for tax.

ONLY THE RICH COULD AFFORD TO TRAVEL LONG DISTANCES

Secondly, in ancient times, traveling long distances when and wherever one likes is a luxury the poor could not afford. Joseph and Mary would have had to travel 90 miles when the couple left their home in Nazareth to register for the census in Bethlehem. This would have been an arduous journey, traveling south along the flatbeds of the Jordan River, then west over the hills surrounding Jerusalem, and on into Bethlehem. It is not a trip that could be done on foot, especially as Mary was heavily pregnant at the time. The journey would have taken almost two weeks and would require them to travel on horses, mules or donkeys, and have plenty of provisions if they were to survive such a grueling journey. Anyone who can make such a trip would most likely hire a guide or travel in a caravan of other travelers such as merchants or with friends and relatives for protection against bandits and robbers. As all of these options required great expense, this was not a journey a poor person was able to make.

We must understand that biblical writers were often *laconic* about certain events because it was always assumed that specific details would be *common knowledge* to the people of that time. So, the nativity story we see depicted every Christmas is far removed from how it really was! From what is revealed later in the book of Luke, traveling in a caravan of relatives and friends was the most likely option Mary and Joseph took. We see the couple traveling in this manner when they brought Jesus to the temple when He was 12 years old.

Now his parents went to Jerusalem every year at the feast of the Passover. And when he was twelve years old, they went up to Jerusalem after the custom of the feast. And when they had fulfilled the days, as they returned, the child Jesus tarried behind in Jerusalem; and Joseph and his mother knew not of it.

But they, supposing him to have been in the company, went a day's journey; and they sought him among their kinsfolk and acquaintance. And when they found him not, they turned back again to Jerusalem, seeking him. And it came to pass, that after three days they found him in the temple, sitting in the midst of the doctors, both hearing them, and asking them questions.

- Luke 2:41-46

So large was their caravan that *a whole day* had passed before they realized the boy Jesus was not among them! This travel arrangement is more characteristic of a wealthy Bedouin family and was certainly not how a poor person would travel. In today's society, this would be comparable to dignitaries or celebrities traveling with a large entourage.

Mary and Joseph traveled in this way every year to attend the feast of the Passover. The feast of the Passover is one of the most important religious festivals in the Jewish calendar. Jews celebrate the Passover *(Pesach in Hebrew)* to commemorate the liberation of the Children of Israel, when they were led out of Egypt by Moses. As Judaism excluded the very poor from the center of religious life, it is implausible that Joseph and Mary would have made such a trip if they were so poor.

THE POOR PERSON'S SACRIFICE

You may be asking,

"IF JOSEPH AND MARY WERE CLASSED AMONGST 'THE HAVES,' WHY DID THEY OFFER A POOR PERSON'S OFFERING DURING THE TIME OF JESUS' DEDICATION?"

The answer is simple - they did not! As mentioned earlier, all but the King James Version of the Bible state that the offering of *'a pair of turtle doves or two young pigeons'* was a provision made for those who could not afford a lamb (Leviticus 12:6-8). The King James Version offers us a more literal translation rather than an interpretation or assumption of what is being said.

Instead of saying, *"If she cannot afford a lamb,"* it simply says,

"If she be not able to bring a lamb, then she shall bring two turtles, or two young pigeons..."

In the Hebrew it says,

"If her hand find not sufficiency of a lamb."

Which could mean: *If a lamb was not available.*

As a very specific lamb was required *(a male lamb in its first year),* it could well be possible that such a lamb may not be readily available to them at the specific time required. So at this point, it is not clear if Leviticus 12:8 refers to a mother not being able to *afford* a lamb.

Fortunately, in another case where a sacrifice is required, the Bible does provide specific details of a **poor person's sacrifice.** This can be found in Leviticus 14, which gives us the sacrificial requirements for those seeking ceremonial purification from a skin disease. Here are the requirements listed in v.10,

- **Two he lambs without blemish**
- One ewe lamb of the first year without blemish
- Three tenth deals of fine flour mingled with oil
- One log of oil

After instructions are given in how the above list should be administered, in v.21, Moses then gives specific instruction for someone who is 'poor' and not able to get all of the above items. Here is the list of items for the poor person's sacrifice:

- **One lamb**
- one tenth deal of fine flour mingled with oil
- A log of oil
- **Two turtledoves, or two young pigeons**

Now let's remind ourselves of what was required for the dedication of a firstborn male: child:

– **One male lamb in its first year,**
or if her hand find not sufficiency for a lamb
– **two turtledoves or two young pigeons.**

As we can see from the list above, a poor person should still be able to afford one lamb. Not only that, but a poor person should also be able to afford two turtledoves or two young pigeons *in addition*. Therefore, what a mother (rich or poor) was required to bring for the dedication of a firstborn male child, *is the same thing a poor person was required to bring*. That being the case, the issue of a mother not being able to bring a lamb has nothing to do with whether she can afford to or not! There must have been other factors as to why she was not able to obtain a lamb at that particular time. Factors that were probably not detailed because they were *common knowledge* to the people of that time.

What is of greater importance is the true significance of the lamb and the requirement to dedicate the firstborn male. That being Christ, who is the reality and the fulfillment of what these things symbolized. All scripture is His personal testimony *(John 5:39)*. Therefore, as God would have it, not only did Mary and Joseph bring two turtledoves or two young pigeons, they also brought *'The Lamb,'* the most important sacrifice of all.

Like Joseph, Daniel, and other prophets before Him, Jesus was born into wealth, not poverty. Joseph was a man of means, known and respected in Judea. Not only as *'The Carpenter,'* but also as *'The Son of David.'* The Jews were waiting for the Messianic King, and they knew he would come from the line of David. Therefore, any son of David would still have ranked within nobility, no matter how many generations had passed.

Jesus was *only* born in humble circumstances because Bethlehem was overcrowded that day, and there was *no room in the inn*. This implies that they first tried to *pay* for lodgings at the inn but it was full. However, by the time the Magi arrived, Mary and Joseph had acquired **a house!**

*When they saw the star, they rejoiced with exceedingly great joy. And when they had come **into the house**, they saw the young Child with Mary His mother, and fell down and worshiped Him.*

- Matthew 2:10-11

CHAPTER 7

A TRIBUTE FOR THE KING

---◆---

And when they had opened their treasures,
they presented unto him gifts…

What is a fitting tribute for a King? More importantly, what is a fitting tribute for the *King of Kings*? A tribute is money or goods paid by kingdoms or countries to acknowledge the superiority of another kingdom. Apart from what was brought to him by merchants and Arabian Kings, Solomon received an annual tribute equating to just under $996 Million in today's economy. That being the case, in keeping with the customs of that time, **where the value of a tribute given to a King or Queen befits their honor and significance,** *should not Jesus receive much more?* After all, He is the King of a Kingdom far superior to any Kingdom of this world! Thankfully, wise men, known as 'Magi,' took up the role of honoring Christ in this way. Unfortunately, various notions regarding these mysterious visitors from the East have obscured the magnitude of what they gave. The traditional Christmas story would have us believe that the wise men's gifts to Jesus comprised of mere *trinkets* consisting of gold, frankincense, and myrrh. Some even say that the value of what they gave would have been enough to finance Jesus, Mary, and Joseph's passage to Egypt, which was necessary to escape Herod's clutches. However, this portrayal can only be part of the many 'absurd traditions and guesses' criticized by M.R. Vincent:

"Many absurd traditions and guesses respecting these visitors to our Lord's cradle have found their way into popular belief and into Christian art. They were said to be kings, and three in number; they were said to be representatives of the three families of Shem, Ham, and Japheth, and therefore one of them is pictured as an Ethiopian; their names are given as Caspar, Balthasar, and Melchior, and their three skulls, said to have been discovered in the twelfth century by Bishop Reinald of Cologne, are exhibited in a priceless casket in the great cathedral of that city."

- Vincent's Word Studies on the New Testament

Despite what you see on Christmas cards and nativity plays, we do not know how many wise men there were. Neither is there any mention of their names throughout scripture. The Bible only says, *"There came wise men from the East."* However, the fact that their entry into Jerusalem sparked panic throughout the whole town indicates that there were far more than just three!

More than likely, the Magi's search for the *'King of the Jews'* resulted from Daniel's influence over them during the time the Jews were taken into captivity by the Babylonians. Not only was he assigned as their master by royal appointment, but they also owed him their lives. King Nebuchadnezzar decreed that all the wise men of Babylon should be destroyed due to their failure to discern the dream that troubled him. However, Daniel, having sought the mercies of God, both revealed and interpreted the King's dream, saving the lives of all Magi. This single event enshrined Daniel in Magian and Babylonian history as Belteshazzar, master of the magicians *(Daniel 4:9)*.

As Daniel was a devout man of God, he most likely would have used his position to share his knowledge of God and the scriptures. As a result, the Magi would undoubtedly have become familiar with the Jewish prophecy of the Messiah.

SO, WHAT WAS THE VALUE OF THE TRIBUTE GIVEN BY THE MAGI?

Although the Bible does not give us a specific amount, we can get an idea of the magnitude of their tribute by knowing more about the Magi themselves. Fortunately, books such as Daniel and the writings of Herodotus and other historians shed more light on these mysterious men from the East.

THE MAGI

The Magi were a tribe of priests from the far East, entrusted with priestly functions similar to the Hebrew tribe of Levi. They were mostly engaged with works related to medicine, astrology, and research into nature. Besides that, they were masters in the art sorcery and divination. It's not surprising that the word "Magi" eventually morphed into "Magic," reflecting their mystical power.

Although the Magi had a pagan heritage, their practices and religious tenets are similar to Judaism. For instance, they practiced monotheism and performed blood sacrifices. The Magi also used bundles of miniature rods in their ceremonies, very similar to the Urim and Thummin the Levitical priests used to seek divine guidance.

However, the power of the Magi was not limited to spiritual matters, for they also had enormous political influence. They held some of the highest ranks in the court of the Babylonian Empire and maintained their lofty positions long after the Medes and Persians conquered Babylon, even in the Parthian Empire.

John MacArthur, a leading pastor, teacher, and author, sheds more light on the political power of the Magi in his Bible Commentary.

"No Persian was ever able to become king without mastering the scientific and religious discipline of the Magi and then being approved and crowned by them."

- The MacArthur New Testament Commentary

According to the book of Esther, when Queen Vashti refused to honor King Ahasuerus's request to present herself to him, the King sought legal counsel from the Magi before giving his verdict on the matter.

"On the seventh day, when the heart of the King was merry with wine, he commanded Mehuman, Biztha, Harbona, Bigtha, Abagtha, Zethar, and Carcas, seven eunuchs who served in the presence of King Ahasuerus, to bring Queen Vashti before the King, wearing her royal crown, in order to show her beauty to the people and the officials, for she was beautiful to behold.

But Queen Vashti refused to come at the King's command brought by his eunuchs; therefore, the King was furious, and his anger burned within him.

*Then the King said to **the wise men** who understood the times (for this was the King's manner toward all who knew law and justice, those closest to him being Carshena, Shethar, Admatha, Tarshish, Meres, Marsena, and Memucan, the seven princes of Persia and Media, who had access to the King's presence, and who ranked highest in the kingdom."*

- Esther 1:10-14

The law of the Medes and Persians was so solemn that it could never be repealed, *not even by the King*. This fact is apparent in the 6th Chapter of Daniel when king Darius' officials duped him into signing a decree that would incontrovertibly sentence Daniel to the lion's den. When the King realized his official's subterfuge, he could do nothing to repeal the order he had made.

Therefore, the fact that King Ahasuerus consulted the Magi about how he could lawfully punish Queen Vashti underscores their influence in the judicial system and the fundamental tenets of the Medo-Persian government. These facts give credence to the claims by some historians that the laws of the Medes and Persian were, in fact, the code of the Magi.

> **Not only was Jesus born into wealth, but by the time He was two, He was already a Billionaire!**

Given the level of power and influence the Magi wielded in the ancient Babylonian and Medo-Persian Empires, one can conclude that they are part of the fraternity that controlled the world in that era. As John MacArthur explains,

"Not only were the Magi responsible for making every monarch that was made in that era, they were also responsible for setting up the judges as well. They had a check system for the despotism that could grow out of a kingship, and so they were the judges that counter-balanced the dictator king."

The eastern empire of the Medes and Persians eventually became the Parthian Empire, where the dominion of the Magi still remained. The Parthian Empire was the only Kingdom that withstood the sprawling Roman Empire. The many wars between the competing empires between 53 BC to 217 AD are more or less a reflection of the present!

By the time the Roman Empire expanded its borders to Mesopotamia, the Parthian Empire was already well-established and wealthy. The

Parthian cities are among the largest in the world. Businesses were prospering with thriving commercial routes into the regions of China. Roman and Parthian borders finally met along the coast of the Mediterranean, Syria, Jordan, Palestine. At the time of Jesus' birth, the Parthians were a significant threat to the Romans and their plans for global dominance. A palpable tension existed in Israel as the power of the East squared off against the power of the West.

Imagine now the impact the Magi made when they came to Jerusalem. These powerful Kingmakers from the east, traveling in full regalia and oriental pomp. Who would have been escorted by a substantial military guard, charging through the city on Persian steed, demanding to see the *'King of the Jews.'* It is no wonder the whole of Jerusalem was in a panic at what initially looked like a Parthian invasion!

Clearly, the Magi were far more than what nativity plays present. They were priests, experts in divination, princes, supreme court judges, and kingmakers, whose influence and power remained intact throughout successive eastern empires!

With all that has been revealed about:

- The Magi's tremendous religious and political power,
- Their deep-seated interest in the prophesied Messiah,
- Plus the fact that in ancient times, a gift from a King or someone of great influence usually amounts to many millions in today's economy...

It is inconceivable to think that the Magi would make such a journey to *honor Jesus* - the King of Kings, with mere trinkets! Not only was their personal guard there for their protection but also to carry the vast treasure trove they brought with them to venerate the divine King of the Jews.

And when they had come into the house, they saw the young Child with Mary His mother, and fell down and worshiped Him. **And when they had opened their treasures,** *they presented gifts to Him: gold, frankincense, and myrrh.*

- Matthew 2:11

To put it in modern-day vernacular, Jesus was *'Set for life!'* Not only was He born into wealth, but by the time He was two, He was already a Billionaire! Although one may argue the validity of such a claim, given that the Bible does not tell us the value of the Magi's gifts, you can be sure that Jesus was far from being poor. You need only look a little closer at His life to see the tell-tale signs of His immense wealth.

CHAPTER 8

JESUS: YOUNG, GIFTED AND RICH

---◆---

"If anyone says to you, 'Why are you doing this?'
say, 'The Lord has need of it"

T he perception of Christ being a poor righteous teacher and healer with *nowhere to lay His head* is the polar opposite to how He was perceived by the people of His day. Jesus was indeed rich, and the perception of Him being poor is an afront to His image! Long before He was seen as *'Messiah,'* the people He lived and walked amongst knew Him as a wealthy young man of royal descent. One only need study His life to see that He moved in the same circles of Israel's wealthy elite. He clearly knew many landowners, and His insight into their personal lives is reflected in the parables He told. However, apart from the miracles He did, what made Jesus so different from the wealthy elite was that **He stood up for the poor.** His message of freedom, power, and prosperity for *'the poor'* was revolutionary. As previously mentioned, poor people were badly treated in Judaean society and were not allowed to participate in the temple's central worship. However, *'the poor'* was the focus of Jesus' message and mission.

"The Spirit of the Lord is upon me, because he has anointed me to preach the gospel to the poor..."

- Luke 4:18

"Blessed are you poor, for yours is the kingdom of God."

- Luke 6:20)

"Go and tell John the things you have seen and heard: that the blind see, the lame walk, the lepers are cleansed, the deaf hear, the dead are raised, the poor have the gospel preached to them."

- Luke 7:22

Jesus saw Himself as a physician, and He went amongst those who needed healing, whether that be in their body, their soul, or in their *finances.* Practically speaking, if you are sick, you won't seek divine healing from someone who has health problems. It is also unlikely that you would take lessons on morality from someone living a sinful life. In the same manner, you would not consider someone advising on prosperity credible unless they themselves were prosperous - spiritually and materially! Jesus was neither sick, immoral, or poor, and His life and ministry on earth were a reflection of that fact.

There is no argument that Jesus lived a sinless life and embodied divine health. However, the fact that He was rich is not so obvious. Mainly because, having been born into wealth, plus receiving a tribute that would see Him *'set for life,'* riches and abundance was a *natural* and seamless part of his life. Therefore, the writers of the four gospels placed no particular emphasis on His wealth, as it was largely taken for granted. It is only the apostle Paul who highlights the fact that Jesus was rich. Not only that, but out of all the things that characterized Jesus, i.e., the healings, the miracles, His sermons, His compassion, His death and resurrection, Paul links *'the grace of our Lord Jesus'* with the fact that He was rich.

*For you know the grace of our Lord Jesus Christ, **that though He was rich, yet for your sake He became poor, so that you through His poverty might become rich.***

- 2 Corinthians 8:9

Many scholars try to *explain* this by saying that Christ was only rich in heaven and then became poor when He lived on earth. However, this could not be further from the truth. As previously mentioned, the only time the virtues of Christ were exchanged for humanity's curse was on the cross. As poverty would undoubtedly have been one of these curses, the only time He became poor was His crucifixion. In addition, the concept of being rich has no significance in heaven because lack and insufficiency do not exist! It is only amid scarcity that one can be considered rich. Therefore, Jesus could only have been rich while on earth, and the atonement He made for *you* to become rich can only be realized during your present existence.

Glimpses of Jesus' wealth can be readily seen through an understanding of the customs of ancient Judaean society. Therefore, with the intent of **restoring Jesus' image**, this chapter attempts to pull back the veil of customary differences between western eyes and ancient Jewish culture so that we may see Jesus as everyone else did at that time. Let us begin at the event where Jesus' first miracle took place.

THE WEDDING AT CANA

On the third day, there was a wedding in Cana of Galilee, and the mother of Jesus was there. Now both Jesus and His disciples were invited to the wedding. And when they ran out of wine, the mother of Jesus said to Him, "They have no wine." Jesus said to her, "Woman, what does your concern have to do with Me? My hour has not yet come." His mother said to the servants, "Whatever He says to you, do it." Now there were set there six waterpots of stone, according to the manner of purification of the Jews, containing twenty or thirty gallons apiece. Jesus said to them, "Fill the waterpots with water." And they filled them up to the brim. And He said to them, "Draw some out now, and take it to the master of the feast." And they took it.

When the master of the feast had tasted the water that was made wine, and did not know where it came from (but the servants who had drawn the water knew), the master of the feast called the bridegroom. And he said to him, "Every man at the beginning sets out the good wine, and when the guests have well drunk, then the inferior. You have kept the good wine until now!" This beginning of signs Jesus did in Cana of Galilee, and manifested His glory; and His disciples believed in Him.

- John 2:1-11

In first-century Jewish culture, wedding feasts were held at the groom's home and were as elaborate as the budget of the house would allow. The six stone waterpots used for purification and ritual washing indicate that this was a large home, as each pot contained 20-30 gallons of water.

A wedding feast typically lasted for a week, and the host would have felt obligated to provide lavish hospitality for the whole duration. Therefore, running out of wine would subject the host's family and the newlyweds to shame and ridicule. Mary was the first to bring the issue of the depleted wine to her son's attention. Maybe because the women's accommodations were near the wine's storage area, she discovered the depleted wine before the men did. Or it could be that the servants approached her first about the issue, and she, in turn, informed Jesus. In either case, as Jesus had not done any miracles up to that point, **their sole reason for coming to Him was for Him to pay for the new supply of wine.**

Although an entire village would gather for a wedding, it was customary for invitees to help pay for expenses. As Jesus and His disciples were *invitees*, it was not out of place for the servants to approach Him for financial aid. *They would not have done so if they did not think it was well within His means to cover such an expense.* Note also that this occurred *before* Jesus was widely known as the Messiah. We know this because He said to Mary, *"My hour has not come yet,"* meaning He was yet to officially start His mission. Therefore, as an invited guest of this wealthy family, His presence at the wedding points to His social standing amongst the Jews.

JESUS HAD SOMEWHERE TO LAY HIS HEAD

One of the reasons why many preachers and scholars suppose that Christ was the poorest of the poor is because of the statement He made to one of His would-be followers:

"Foxes have holes and birds of the air have nests, but the Son of Man has nowhere to lay His head."

- Luke 9:58

"DID JESUS REALLY HAVE NOWHERE TO LAY HIS HEAD, OR WAS HE SPEAKING HYPOTHETICALLY?"

I believe the latter to be true. The book of Matthew tells us that when Jesus heard that John had been put in prison, He left Nazareth and *dwelt* in Capernaum, a coastal town in the region of Zebulun *(Matthew 4:12-13).* Then after this, two of John's disciples (Simon and Andrew) started to follow Jesus after hearing their mentor say, *"Behold the Lamb of God!"* When they asked Jesus, *"Where He was staying?"* He replied, *"Come and see!"* Not only did they see where He was staying, but they also *abode* with Him that day *(John 1:34-39).*

So, Jesus had His own place, where He *laid His head!*
A home suitable enough to entertain guests.

For Simon and Andrew to ask Jesus where He was staying implies that He appeared to be a person of means, who would undoubtedly have His own house or lodgings. Apart from His popularity as a teacher and healer, Jesus' wealth could have well been the underline reason why some would-be followers wanted to join Him. We know Judas was using his position as treasurer to profiteer from Jesus. Also, Jesus made it clear that *not everyone that calls Him Lord shall enter into the Kingdom of heaven (Matthew 7:21).* Therefore, not everyone who followed Jesus did so for genuine reasons. Many may have been attracted to *'what He had'* instead of by *'Who He was.'* Then disappear, when the going got tough! Indeed, this is what many of His disciples did when His teaching got too hard for them to bear. Only eleven dedicated disciples stayed (Judas omitted) because of who He was - **'The Christ, the Son of the living God'** (John 6:66-69).

As Jesus was very adept in knowing a person's heart, the statement, *"Foxes have holes and birds of the air have nests, but the Son of Man has nowhere to lay His head,"* could well be His way of telling this would-be follower not to expect the comfortable life he thinks he would have in following Him.

Jesus,' *'Nowhere to lay my head'* statement could also have been a prophetic one, pointing towards His death on the cross. It was ultimately on the cross, where He would have nowhere to lay His head, as His head and body slumped downward, causing a violent struggle to stand upwards on His nailed feet, in what must have been a desperate effort to breathe. What we know for sure is that **Jesus had**

a place to lay His head, whether at His seafront home in Capernaum or His family home in Nazareth.

"THE LORD HAS NEED OF IT"

Another sign of Jesus' wealth is unveiled in His triumphant entry into Jerusalem. In preparation for this, Jesus instructed two of His disciples to:

*"Go into the village opposite you; and as soon as you have entered it you will find a colt tied, **on which no one has sat.** Loose it and bring it. And if anyone says to you, 'Why are you doing this?' say, 'The Lord has need of it,' and immediately he will send it here."*

- Mark 11:2-3

It may be difficult to see any significance in what was happening here to modern western eyes, as the disciples are merely fetching a young donkey for Jesus to ride on. *"What's the big deal in that?"* However, as indicated by the attention the disciples received, from the men demanding why they were taking the colt, *this was a very big deal!*

In order to grasp the significance of this, I want you to imagine being in London, and as you walked along the street, you came across a Bentley. But this was no ordinary Bentley - it was the Bentley State Limousine! The Bentley State Limousine is the official state car for Her Majesty Queen Elizabeth II, created for her Golden Jubilee in 2002. Only two were built, and each has an estimated value of $500,000. Even if you did not know it belonged to the Queen, its illuminated coat-of-arms and a pennant mounted on the roof makes it clear that it belongs to *royalty*. You also know that there is no way you can approach such a car without attracting the attention of security! This is the same scenario the disciples were presented with. In this ancient culture, a colt was the mount of Kings! Especially one that had never been ridden before.

The colt, therefore, was the State Limousine of that time and place. Only royalty or someone of great prestige and wealth could *own* one. To the people of that time, seeing someone riding this colt would have been more meaningful than us seeing a celebrity in a stretch limousine. When Jesus was seen riding on that colt through the streets of Jerusalem, it is very likely that they took this as a sign, He was going to overthrow the Romans and take His place as their rightful King!

According to the original Greek text, when Jesus told the disciple to say, *"The Lord has need of it,"* what this actually meant was that *'The Owner'* has need of it. The fact that the men *(who were probably hired to guard the colt)* accepted the disciples' explanation means that it was very plausible for them to believe that JESUS was its rightful owner.

JESUS HAD FINANCIAL BACKERS

In addition to the tribute He received at birth, Jesus had financial backers! Like Elisha and the prophets before Him, He received a great value of gifts and money from individuals He had healed.

And certain women, which had been healed of evil spirits and infirmities, Mary called Magdalene, out of whom went seven devils, and Joanna the wife of Chuza Herod's steward, and Susanna, and many others, which ministered unto him of their substance.

- Luke 8:2-3

It is important to note that Jesus did not *need* financial support from anyone, nor would He have asked them for money. As mentioned earlier, it was customary for those who were wealthy to give generously to the *man of God* out of gratitude for divine healing. This is certainly what these women and others did when Jesus delivered them from their infirmities.

From what we can glean from the scriptures, it would appear these were very wealthy women. Joanna, whose name meant *'Jehovah is a gracious giver,'* was the wife of Chuza. Chuza, whose name meant *'The Seer,'* was the steward of King Herod Antipas and would have managed the King's properties. Not only would he have managed Herod's properties, but as his chief-of-staff and a man of great insight, the King would have trusted Chuza with all his affairs. Therefore, Joanna and her husband held a high position in the Judaean social strata.

Little is mentioned about Susanna except for her close association with Joanna. She may have been amongst *'the other women'* who visited Jesus' tomb after His resurrection, alongside Joanna, Mary Magdalene, and Mary, the mother of James. With her close link to Joanna, and given the vast socioeconomic divides between *'The Haves'* and *'The Have nots,'* Susanna was very likely ranked amongst the wealthy elite.

Mary Magdalene was arguably the most controversial of the women who supported Jesus. Although branded 'a sinner' by the religious leaders of her day, her devotion to Jesus was unparalleled. Not only did she anoint Jesus' head with spikenard oil *(worth $36,000 in today's economy)*, but just four days prior, she anointed His feet with the same costly oil.

Then Jesus six days before the Passover came to Bethany, where Lazarus was which had been dead, whom he raised from the dead. There they made him a supper; and Martha served: but Lazarus was one of them that sat at the table with him. Then took Mary a pound of ointment of spikenard, very costly, and anointed the feet of Jesus, and wiped his feet with her hair: and the house was filled with the odour of the ointment.

- John 12:1-3

There can be no doubt that Mary was a woman of means who gave *lavishly* to Jesus. Judging from the tomb her brother, Lazarus, was buried in *(before being raised from the dead)*, a tomb very similar to the one owned by Joseph of Arimathea, Mary also belonged to a family ranked amongst the wealthy elite of that day. Jesus' close relationship with her family sheds some light on the social circles He moved in.

THE MONEY BAG

With all the financial backing Jesus received on top of His personal fortune, *He had need of a treasurer!* That role was given to Judas, who was entrusted to carry His *money bag*. Unfortunately, Judas was a thief, who helped himself to what was put in the bag *(John 12:6)*. The fact that he managed to pilfer Jesus' money, for such a long time, is an indication of how much money there was.

"SO, HOW MUCH MONEY WAS IN THE BAG?"

Although the Bible never states how much money was in the bag at any given time, Jesus' *'spending power'* was quite considerable. On the night before the feast of Passover, the night of Jesus' betrayal, Jesus said to Judas, *"What you do, do quickly."* As Judas had the money bag, the other disciples thought Jesus had instructed him to go and buy what was needed for the forthcoming 'Feast of the Passover' or to give something to the poor. For the other disciples to make that assumption implies that giving to the poor and providing for the disciple's needs was quite routine. Although not stated, it is very likely that family members also accompanied the 12 disciples and their financial needs were also met. This could well have been the case during the time Jesus had 72 disciples in His company!

When the disciples asked where they would eat the Passover meal, Mark 14 indicates that Jesus had already *booked* a large upper room at an inn, under the name, *'The Teacher.'*

*Now on the first day of Unleavened Bread, when they killed the Passover lamb, His disciples said to Him, **"Where do You want us to go and prepare, that You may eat the Passover?"***

And He sent out two of His disciples and said to them, "Go into the city, and a man will meet you carrying a pitcher of water; follow him. Wherever he goes in, say to the master of the house, '

The Teacher says, "Where is the guest room in which I may eat the Passover with My disciples?" '

Then he will show you a large upper room, furnished and prepared; there make ready for us." So His disciples went out, and came into the city, and found it just as He had said to them; and they prepared the Passover.

- Mark 14:12-16

Jesus' day-to-day expenditure was high. However, whether He was covering the cost for seventy-two disciples or the twelve, there was still enough money in the bag to buy food for well over 5000 people in one sitting!

*When the day was now far spent, His disciples came to Him and said, "This is a deserted place, and already the hour is late. Send them away, that they may go into the surrounding country and villages and buy themselves bread; for they have nothing to eat." But He answered and said to them, "You **give them** something to eat." And they said to Him,*

"Shall we go and buy two hundred denarii worth of bread and give them something to eat?"

- Mark 6:35-37

Although Jesus never told the disciples to *buy* something to eat, that is exactly what *they thought* He meant. Their question of whether to buy 200 denarii of bread ($24,000 in today's economy) was not sarcasm, as some may suggest, but a serious one. As a matter of fact, the Wuest Expanded translation of the New Testament informs us that they had already started going when they asked Jesus that question. So, although Jesus supernaturally fed the 5000 *(in addition to the women and children who were not counted in that number)*, it was well within His means to buy food for them all!

THEY DIVIDED UP HIS CLOTHES

Another indication of Jesus' wealth was at His crucifixion, where four soldiers competed for His clothes.

When the soldiers crucified Jesus, they took his clothes, dividing them into four shares, one for each of them, with the undergarment remaining. This garment was seamless, woven in one piece from top to bottom. "Let's not tear it," they said to one another. "Let's decide by lot who will get it." This happened that the scripture might be fulfilled that said, "They divided my clothes among them and cast lots for my garment." So this is what the soldiers did.

- John 19:23-24

It is doubtful that the Roman soldiers would have divided up Jesus' clothes if they were not anything of value. Although Jesus would not have been wearing the long flowing robes the Pharisees liked to show-off in, that does not mean He did not wear quality. Ancient Judaean dresswear comprised of an outer garment and undergarments. The outer garment would have been the *simlāh*, a large rectangular piece of rough, heavy woolen material *(though sometimes linen)* crudely sewed together so that the front was unstitched and with two openings for the arms. However, the Roman soldiers were not interested in the form of clothing Christ wore, just *the material* it was made of. That is why the garments were torn into four shares. As Roman clothing was commonly made of wool, Jesus' outer garment was likely made of the more expensive linen imported from Egypt. Only wealthy Romans could afford linen tunics, so the soldiers would have undoubtedly seized the opportunity to have linen tunics made using Jesus' attire.

The undergarment the soldiers drew lots for was also made from linen; however, this time, it was the *form* of clothing that was of greater value. Jesus' undergarment was a *seamless* garment woven in one piece from top to bottom. This seamless tunic would have taken remarkable skill and ingenuity to make, not something the average layperson could afford to buy. As Roman citizens wore tunics as an outer garment, this seamless tunic would have been quite a prize, giving a semblance of prestige and status when worn in Rome.

CONCLUSION

To the people whom Jesus lived amongst, it was no secret that He was rich! His social standing within Judaean society squarely places Him amongst *'The Haves,'* rather than the *'Have nots!'* Born into nobility as a son of David, He attended the weddings of wealthy landowning families and was often invited to dine in their homes. Unlike the very poor, who were excluded from the center of religious life, Jesus had unfettered access to the temple and synagogues from an early age, where He conversed with preeminent doctors and teachers of the law. Among other things, He owned a seafront house in Capernaum as well as a donkey and colt - *the luxury cars of that era!* Jesus lived life abundantly - the very life He wants us to live (John 10:10).

That being the case, the very notion of Christ being amongst the poorest of the poor is a lie. *Jesus was rich!* His birth was marked by the treasure trove He received from the mighty Magi, and His death saw Roman soldiers squabbling over His clothes!

Even Jesus' disciples became rich because of Him! For, what do you think they did with the great multitude of fish they caught at Jesus' command? A haul so great that it filled two ships, and both began to sink *(Luke 5:4-9)*. The answer is simple. They sold the fish and became rich! That is probably why Simon Peter felt so *'unworthy'* to receive so great a catch, telling Jesus to *"Depart from me for I am a sinful man!"* He was obviously overwhelmed by the unmerited advent of *sudden wealth*. After that life-changing event, they were all able to retire from the fishing business and follow Jesus!

No doubt, some of you will remind me that it was Christ Himself who said,

"It is easier for a camel to go through the eye of a needle than for a rich man to enter the kingdom of God."

However, as I will discuss later, the statements made against *'the rich'* throughout scripture have been grossly misconstrued as an endorsement to live a life void of earthly possessions. The so-called virtues of poverty go against *'the gospel of the Kingdom'* - the gospel that Jesus preached - of a heavenly dimension of unlimited power and resources, by which one can manifest the good that they desire, if only they believe.

BOOK 2

MIND
BEFORE
MATTER

THE MYSTERIES OF THE KINGDOM OF HEAVEN

———————◆———————

To truly understand the teachings and the nature of the Bible, you must first understand the teachings and nature of Christ as demonstrated in His earthly ministry.

In the beginning was the Word, and the Word was with God, and the Word was God. He was in the beginning with God. All things were made through Him, and without Him nothing was made that was made. In Him was life, and the life was the light of men.

- John 1:1-4

Jesus *is* the Word, the Word that was with God, and the Word who is God. He is the Word that became flesh and dwelt amongst us *(John 1:14)*. The Bible also declares that He came in *'the volume of the book that is written of Him' (Hebrews 10:7)*. Therefore, every book in the Bible points to Christ!

SO, WHAT IS IT THAT WE CAN LEARN ABOUT THE BIBLE FROM LOOKING AT JESUS?

Well, one of the most notable things about Jesus is that He often spoke in parables.

All these things Jesus spoke to the multitude in parables; **and without a parable He did not speak to them,** *that it might be fulfilled which was spoken by the prophet, saying: "I will open* **My mouth in parables;** *I will utter things kept secret from the foundation of the world."*

- Matthew 13:34-35

THE MYSTERY IN PARABLES

The Greek word for parable is *'Parabole,'* which means placing one thing by another's side. Parables present one story, with two meanings or versions, placed side by side. There is the *exoteric* - the literal, or *'outer'* meaning, and then there is the *esoteric* - the spiritual or *'inner'* meaning. The exoteric version or meaning is the one that is suitable to be imparted to the crowd. It is the meaning that is most *obvious* to the casual hearer. On the other hand, the esoteric is the true meaning, or what I like to call the *'power meaning.'* It is the meaning that is not so obvious, given to those with the mind to put into *practice* the teachings of Christ.

When Jesus spoke to the multitude, He spoke in parables, but when He was alone with His disciples, **He explained all things to them** *(Mark 4:34)*. Therefore, the outer meaning is for the *'spectator,'* or *'hearer of the word,'* whereas the inner or power meaning is for *'disciples,'* *'practitioners,'* or *'doers of the word.'*

The purpose of the outer meaning is to help the practitioner *visualize* the dynamics of the inner version. Without the external understanding, the inner version may not make much sense. Therefore, for the practitioner or *'doer of the word,'* both outer and inner versions are required. The spectator, on the other hand, need only concern him or herself with the outer *(literal)* meaning. The book of James makes a clear distinction between *'hearers of the word'* and *'doers of the word,'*

*Be doers of the Word, and not hearers only, deceiving yourselves. For if anyone is a hearer of the Word and not a doer, **he is like a man observing his natural face in a mirror;** for he observes himself, goes away, and immediately forgets what kind of man he was. But he who looks into the perfect law of liberty and continues in it, and is not a forgetful hearer but a doer of the work, this one will be blessed in what he does.*

- James 1:22-25

YOUR DIVINE IDENTITY

The fact that the *'hearer of the Word'* is like a man observing his natural face in the mirror points to our *divine identity*. God and His Word are one! As such, seeing your true face in the Word can only mean that you are a *reflection* of God. To hear the Word but not *do* the Word is to reject one's own identity. Jesus came to *remind you* of the person you really are, and if you are willing to embrace the truth, then it is given to you to know the **mysteries of the Kingdom of heaven.**

*And the disciples came and said to Him [Jesus], "Why do You speak to them in parables?" He answered and said to them, "Because it has been given to you to know the mysteries of the Kingdom of heaven, **but to them it has not been given."***

- Matthew 13:10-11

UNLOCKING THE MYSTERY

The true meaning of the Word, is hidden from the crowd and casual observer, while at the same time, revealed to those who desire to practice what Christ preached. To practice what Jesus preached, you need to understand the mysteries of the Kingdom of heaven [the secrets of our divine nature]. The keys to understanding these mysteries can only be found in many of the esoteric or *'disciple's version'* of the parables. However, there is one parable in particular that unravels the mysteries of the Kingdom when it is rightly understood. That is *the parable of the sower.*

But when He was alone, those around Him with the twelve asked Him about the parable [of the sower]... And He said to them, "Do you not understand this parable? **How then will you understand all the parables?**

- Mark 4:10 and 13

When Jesus said, *"All parables,"* we should not limit this to the parables told in the four gospels, but to the entire Bible! As mentioned, Jesus came in the [full] volume of the book, written of Him. As both old and new testament Scripture reflects the character and nature of Christ, His use of parables informs us that the entire Bible is a parable, made up of parables. Unlocking the Bible's mysteries reveals Christ, and a revelation of Christ is a revelation of your true identity.

SO, WHAT ARE THE KEYS EMBEDDED IN THIS PARABLE, BY WHICH WE CAN PERCEIVE THE BIBLE IN ITS TRUE LIGHT?

As mentioned, the outer version of a parable helps the practitioner visualize the dynamics of the inner meaning. So, let us begin with what was told to *the crowd*.

"Behold, a sower went out to sow. And as he sowed, some seed fell by the wayside; and the birds came and devoured them. Some fell on stony places, where they did not have much earth; and they immediately sprang up because they had no depth of earth. But when the sun was up they were scorched, and because they had no root they withered away. And some fell among thorns, and the thorns sprang up and choked them. But others fell on good ground and yielded a crop: some a hundredfold, some sixty, some thirty."

- Matthew 13:4-8

Now here is the esoteric or *'disciple's version'* of the same parable:

"When anyone hears the Word of the Kingdom and does not understand it, then the wicked one comes and snatches away what was sown in his heart. This is he who received seed by the wayside.

But he who received the seed on stony places, this is he who hears the Word and immediately receives it with joy; yet he has no root in himself, but endures only for a while. For when tribulation or persecution arises because of the Word, immediately he stumbles.

Now he who received seed among the thorns is he who hears the Word, and the cares of this world and the deceitfulness of riches choke the Word, and he becomes unfruitful. But he who received seed on the good ground is he who hears the Word and understands it, who indeed bears fruit and produces: some a hundredfold, some sixty, some thirty."

- Matthew 13:19-23

The key elements in the parable of the sower are **the sower, the seed, the soil,** and **the fruit.** All the components required for sowing and reaping! Many of the parables Jesus told involved the sower, the seed, the soil, and fruit, in various forms and permutations. Whether it be…

- The Weeds Among the Wheat *(Matthew 13:24-30)*
- The Mustard Seed *(Matthew 13:31-32)*
- The Leaven *(Matthew 13:33-34)*
- Hidden Treasure *(Matthew 13:44)*
- Laborers in the Vineyard *(Matthew 20:1-16)*
- The Tenant Farmers *(Matthew 21:33-45)*

… all carry a sense of sowing and reaping.

According to the disciple's version of the parable of the sower:

- The sower is God.
- The seed is God's thoughts.
- The soil is the heart (the subconscious mind).
- The fruit is the manifestation of thought sown in the heart.

THE POWER OF YOUR MIND

When thoughts are sown into the fertile soil of the subconscious mind, they *manifest* into physical reality. The various soils or grounds are conditions of the heart. **Only one heart condition** 'bears fruit,' that being the mind that hears, understands, believes, and accepts the Word as *truth*. Once that thought has been accepted as truth, it is only a matter of time before it materializes into physical reality. This is the divine law of the mind!

To the heart or subconscious mind, there is no difference between physical and mental actions. What you imagine yourself doing or achieving is just as real as if you were physically doing it. *What is real in your heart will be real in your life.* The only difference between mental reality and the equivalent physical reality is 'time.' Therefore, what you believe in your mind should be taken more seriously than what takes place in physical reality. That certainly was the perspective Jesus had. That is why He said,

"You have heard that it was said to those of old, 'You shall not murder, and whoever murders will be in danger of the judgment.' But I say to you that whoever is angry with his brother without a cause shall be in danger of the judgment"
- Matthew 5:21-22

"You have heard that it was said to those of old, 'You shall not commit adultery.' But I say to you that whoever looks at a woman to lust for her has already committed adultery with her in his heart"

- Matthew 5:27-28

To the degree that you believe something to be true is to the degree that you will manifest that 'truth' - 'some a hundredfold, some sixty, some thirty.' That is why Jesus often said, *"According to your faith be it unto you."*

THE MYSTERIES OF THE KINGDOM PERTAIN TO THE MIND'S ABILITY TO MANIFEST THOUGHT.

HERE LIES THE SECRET OF YOUR DIVINE NATURE.

If this is the fundamental meaning behind the parable of the sower, then all parables, and indeed, **all scripture should be seen through the lens of the mind's ability to manifest God's thoughts.** This is the only means by which you can be *'fruitful'* and manifest the Kingdom as Christ did.

God's first commandment to man was to *"Be fruitful and multiply."* When He said this, He was not talking about procreation *(that was the second command)* but instead, using your mind to manifest the good that you desire, and your mouth to *'call those things that be not, as if they were' (Romans 4:17).* That is how the will of God is done on the earth. That being the case, the principles, lessons, and promises in the Bible must pertain to how we manage our thoughts.

We are, in essence, *beings of thought* endowed with the ability to manifest **God's thoughts**. God is good, and His thoughts are good! Thoughts of joy, peace, success, freedom, health, and wealth. Thoughts to prosper you and not to harm you, to give you hope and a future.

Jesus is the *true vine*, and we are the branches in the vine *(John 15:1-8)*. The life of the vine flows into the branches. As branches, we are to express the life of the vine as fruit! The life of the vine is 'God's thoughts,' and the fruit is the manifestation of His thoughts, expressed as the good that we desire. Hence, Jesus said,

"If you abide in Me, and My words abide in you, you will ask what you desire, and it shall be done for you. By this My Father is glorified, that you bear much fruit; so you will be My disciples."

- John 15:1-8

Therefore, our primary purpose is to manifest *the good that we desire*, not just for our benefit but also for the well-being of others.

• You are only a disciple of Christ when you bear much fruit, that being, the goodness that stems from God's thoughts.

• Your Heavenly Father is glorified when you bear much fruit.

• If you are not manifesting God's goodness (success, joy, freedom, peace, prosperity, health, and wealth), you are neither fruitful nor a disciple of Christ!

• It is God's good pleasure for you to have what you desire, through Christ's mind **in you**. The creative power through which all things were made.

Overall, the teachings of Christ tell us that,

'Mind comes before matter,'

and materiality is the product of that which is spiritual. Therefore, manifesting God's thoughts and the good that one desires is what spirituality and successful living is all about!

———◆———

CHAPTER 9

THE LESSON FOR THE RICH YOUNG RULER

PART ONE

"How hard it is for those who have riches to enter the kingdom of God"

If Jesus was so rich, why does Christianity portray Him as poor and destitute, with nothing but the clothes on His back? - Part of the reason could be that, like God's leading servants, Jesus' character, gifts, and qualities far outshone His wealth. The fact that He was rich was *'incidental,'* the same way it should be for all who embrace the good news of the Kingdom! However, the main reason seems to lie squarely upon how the story of *the rich young ruler* has been interpreted.

Now as He was going out on the road, one came running, knelt before Him, and asked Him, "Good Teacher, what shall I do that I may inherit eternal life?" So Jesus said to him, "Why do you call Me good? No one is good but One, that is, God. You know the commandments: 'Do not commit adultery,' 'Do not murder,' 'Do not steal,' 'Do not bear false witness,' 'Do not defraud,' 'Honor your father and your mother.'

"And he answered and said to Him, "Teacher, all these things I have kept from my youth." Then Jesus, looking at him, loved him, and said to him,

*"One thing you lack: **Go your way, sell whatever you have and give to the poor, and you will have treasure in heaven; and come, take up the cross, and follow Me."***

But he was sad at this word, and went away sorrowful, for he had great possessions.** Then Jesus looked around and said to His disciples, **"How hard it is for those who have riches to enter the kingdom of God!"

- Mark 10:17-22

Contrary to traditional belief, when Jesus told the young man to sell what he had and give to the poor, He was addressing his *specific* problem. It is not an instruction or doctrine that pertains to everyone!

This is a crucial distinction because the stance taken by many in the church on:

- The virtue of poverty
- The renunciation of material wealth
- The institutionalization of poverty in the priesthood
- and the view that those who do not practice poverty are void of Christ's Spirit,

...rests upon Christ's discourse with the rich young ruler.

Like Jesus, this man was also young, rich, and powerful. The consensus amongst Christian commentators is that the story of the rich young ruler is a teaching on the detrimental effect money and material wealth can have on one's desire for eternal life. Indeed, this young man *(who was very likely a Pharisee given that the Sadducees did not believe in the afterlife)* was sincere in his pursuit of righteousness and even considered himself *faultless* regarding the law. However, being asked to sell all his possessions and follow Jesus was a price too high!

It is, therefore, assumed that if the young man had loved God more than money, he would have been willing to sell what He had and follow Jesus. But instead, because he was rich, he clung to his possessions and *'lost out'* on eternal life! Based on this notion, Jesus rightly said,

"How hard it is for those who have riches to enter the kingdom of God! For it is easier for a camel to go through the eye of a needle than for a rich man to enter the kingdom of God."

Not only did Jesus masterfully prove that this young man was *not* faultless concerning the law, He also exposed the *greed* that was in his heart. **The same greed that resides in all that are rich!** Therefore, being rich and having great possessions prevents you from entering the Kingdom of God because you are less likely to give up these things to follow Jesus.

However…

IS THIS REALLY WHAT THIS STORY IS ABOUT?

IS THE DETRIMENTAL EFFECT MONEY CAN HAVE ON ONE'S DESIRE FOR ETERNAL LIFE THE TRUE LESSON TO LEARN FROM JESUS' DISCOURSE WITH THE RICH YOUNG RULER?

DOES BEING RICH MEAN THAT YOU ARE GREEDY?

OR…

IS THERE A MORE PROFOUND LESSON TO BE LEARNED?

These are the questions I would like you to consider before lambasting and passing judgement on the rich young ruler. Because if he failed to inherit the Kingdom for refusing to give *all* that he had, then by this argument, what is the fate awaiting the multitude of Christians who fail to give a tenth of their income to their church? It would also be the height of naivety to believe that only the rich would fail to comply, if the same charge to *'sell one's possessions and give to the poor,'* was directed to *all* believers. Indeed, the middle class and those with moderate incomes would also fail to meet this request. The same fundamental issue the rich young ruler had is the same issue that we all have in varying degrees.

IS GREED AND THE LOVE OF MONEY THE REAL ISSUE, OR IS IT SOMETHING ELSE?

It is indeed *something else,'* and understanding the problem is key to unravelling why Jesus told the rich young ruler to sell what he had and give to the poor. To find out what it is, **we need to interpret Jesus' instruction to the rich young ruler in the** *context* **of His overall teaching.** With that in mind, let us begin our journey with the occasion when Jesus warned His disciples to **beware the leaven of the Pharisees and Sadducees.**

CHAPTER 10

BEWARE THE LEAVEN OF THE PHARISEES

"You know how to discern the face of the sky,
but you cannot discern the signs of the times"

Now when His disciples had come to the other side, they had forgotten to take bread. Then Jesus said to them, **"Take heed and beware of the leaven of the Pharisees and the Sadducees."** And they reasoned among themselves, saying, "It is because we have taken no bread." But Jesus, being aware of it, said to them,

"O you of little faith, why do you reason among yourselves because you have brought no bread? Do you not yet understand, or remember the five loaves of the five thousand and how many baskets you took up? Nor the seven loaves of the four thousand and how many large baskets you took up? How is it you do not understand that I did not speak to you concerning bread? - but to beware of the leaven of the Pharisees and Sadducees."

*Then they understood that He did not tell them to beware of the leaven of bread, but of **the doctrine of the Pharisees and Sadducees.***

- Matthew 16:5-12

Just prior to this moment, Jesus rebuked the Pharisees and Sadducees for asking Him for a sign from heaven.

*Then the Pharisees and Sadducees came, and testing Him asked that He would show them a sign from heaven. He answered and said to them, "When it is evening you say, 'It will be fair weather, for the sky is red'; and in the morning, 'It will be foul weather today, for the sky is red and threatening.' **Hypocrites! You know how to discern the face of the sky, but you cannot discern the signs of the times.***

- Matthew 16:1-3

Jesus called the religious leaders *'hypocrites,'* because they knew how to discern the *face of the sky,* but failed to *discern* the signs of the times. In other words, they knew how to recognize *outward signs* that was *apparent* to all, but as Israel's Spiritual leaders, lacked the discernment required to understand the *sign of the times* or what was taking place *spiritually*. Jesus calls those who rely on outward signs to guide their lives a *'wicked and adulterous generation.'* This was the reason why He told His disciples to beware of the *doctrine* of Pharisees and Sadducees.

- A doctrine based on the limitations of the outer physical world, rather than the infinite possibilities of *your* inner spiritual reality.

- A doctrine based on facts rather than truth.

- A doctrine that prides outward appearance over inner qualities.

To explain this further, let me first present to you a basic illustration of reality.

INNER AND OUTER WORLD BASICS

In the Bible, the universe is described as the Heavens and the Earth. Heaven is the realm of God's mind, presence, and reality. It is the inner spiritual world, whereas the earth represents the physical outer world. The outer world is the visible world rooted in an invisible world, that being spiritual. When we look at a plant, we know there is more to it than what we can see because its roots are hidden in the earth. This is a simplified analogy of the universe: the unseen spiritual realm coexisting with the visible physical world.

When I say *'spiritual,'* I am not talking about religion or any particular faith. Instead, I am referring to that which is *intangible* but very real. For

> ## The invisible realm is the realm of vision

example, your thoughts are intangible but very real. Love is intangible but real. Faith is intangible but real. On the other end of the spectrum, fear and hate are intangible but very real. None of these can be seen in their pure form in the physical world; we can only see or experience the manifestation of these things.

Although the inner world is the invisible realm, it is the realm of *vision*. The outer world is the manifestation of what is seen in the inner world. Hebrews 11:3 and 2 Corinthian 4:18 address this concept succinctly. When the two scriptures are read *as one*, it gives us the true nature of our world.

Through faith, we understand that the worlds were framed by the word of God, so that things which are seen were not made of things which do appear. While we look not at the things which are seen, but at the things which are not seen: for the things which are seen are temporal; but the things which are not seen are eternal.

Simply put;

• Things which are seen [tangible things] are made from things which are not seen [intangible things].

Even science agrees that when matter is broken down to the *subatomic level*, all you are left with is energy.

• Tangible things are temporal, changeable and finite.

• Intangible things are eternal, unchangeable and infinite.

If tangible things are made from intangible things,

And...

Intangible things are eternal, but tangible things are temporal...

...then it stands to reason that **intangible things are more powerful than tangible things.** This is the complete opposite from what we have been *conditioned* to believe.

THE KINGDOM WITHIN

I call the heavens the *'inner world'* because, contrary to common thinking, heaven is a dimension experienced from *within.* One of the most profound statements Jesus made was that *the Kingdom of God is within you!*

Now when He was asked by the Pharisees when the kingdom of God would come, He answered them and said, "The kingdom of God does not come with observation; nor will they say, 'See here!' or 'See there!' For indeed, the kingdom of God is within you."

- Luke 17:20-21

God's Kingdom *is not in the sky* or anywhere in your outer world. The Kingdom of God, His mind, presence and reality is *within you!* We are more spiritual than physical. More infinite than finite. More divine than human. **Heaven is your inner world.** Unfortunately, many of us live a life so immersed in the theater of physical reality that we are unaware of the immense power, wisdom, and infinite possibilities that lie within. The *'God realm'* is within you. That is why the Bible is full of examples where He speaks to men and women from the inner sanctum of *dreams and visions.* Paul wrote of a dramatic experience where he was *'caught up'* to the **'third heaven.'** An experience so real, he could not tell if he was in his body or not!

It is doubtless not profitable for me to boast. **I will come to visions and revelations of the Lord:** *I know a man in Christ who fourteen years ago - whether in the body I do not know, or whether out of the body I do not know, God knows - such a one was caught up to the third heaven. And I know such a man - whether in the body or out of the body I do not know, God knows - how he was caught up into Paradise and heard inexpressible words, which it is not lawful for a man to utter.*

- 2 Corinthians 12:1-7

Although Paul could not tell if he was in his body or not, everything he experienced was in the context of *visions and revelations.* Over 50 dreams are discussed in Scripture, and when people awoke, they acted on these dreams.

For God may speak in one way, or in another, yet man does not perceive it. In a dream, in a vision of the night, when deep sleep falls upon men, while slumbering on their beds, then He opens the ears of men, and seals their instruction.

- Job 33:14

God is still in the business of revealing things through dreams and visions, and although they are but a brief foray into the spiritual realm, at that moment, you can see something so profound, it can change the world.

Take for example, the 22-year-old University of Michigan graduate who was struck in the middle of the night with a vision. He had somehow managed to download the entire Web and just keep the links. He immediately grabbed a pen when he awoke and wrote down what became the basis for an algorithm. He used this algorithm to power a new Web search engine. That young graduate was Larry Page, and the search engine he saw in a vision became Google. Today Larry Page is one of the richest men in the world with a net worth of $82 Billion. His visionary experience is just one of countless examples of how the world has been shaped by what is revealed in visions and dreams.

MIND COMES BEFORE MATTER

We were all created to be visionaries - *individuals with the ability to visualize and manifest the future we desire.* As such, our primary function in life is to manifest into outer reality what we see in our inner world. As mentioned earlier,

'THINGS WHICH ARE SEEN ARE MADE FROM THINGS WHICH ARE NOT SEEN.'

When Paul talks about *'things which are not seen'* he is referring to that which can only be seen on the screen of our **imagination**. Sight is the faculty of the mind, not the eyes. Your physical eyes serve only as a window that gives one dimension of sight. However, it is your mind that gives meaning to the streams of light and colors that pass through your eyes. Your imagination, or what is also called *'the eyes of your understanding,'* are your *real eyes,* enabling you to see things that your physical eyes cannot.

Strangely enough, Paul adjures us *not* to look at *things seen*, only the things that are *not seen*. God does not want your focus to be set on how things appear or what has *already* been manifested. He wants you to focus on the things to come *(John 16:13)*.

Some may misconstrue this to mean that God does not want us to have material wealth and possessions, but that is certainly not the case. Material possessions are for our use and enjoyment. It is also a means by which we can do good to others. However, **an inordinate focus on what can be seen with your eyes, dulls or weakens your ability to see what God wants to reveal to your mind!** That, in turn, limits your ability to manifest the good that you desire. Hence the Proverb,

*Where there is no vision, the people perish: but **he that keeps the law**, happy is he.*

- Proverbs 29:18 KJV

"WHAT IS THE LAW THAT ONE SHOULD KEEP?"

It is the law of the mind! What must be understood is that *'Mind comes before matter.'* Material things are the fruit of what is first seen in the mind. Anything you want to achieve in life must be manifested through your mind. The airplane had to be first seen in the mind before it could be flown in the sky. The automobile was first seen in the mind before driven on the road. Everything around us is the product of what was first seen in the mind. There is a well known saying,

**"If you can see it in your mind,
you will hold it in your hand."**

BUYING WITHOUT MONEY

The fact that material things are the product of what is first seen in the mind is the reason why God invites us to *buy without money!*

Everyone who thirsts, come to the waters; And you who have no money, come, buy and eat. Yes, come, buy wine and milk without money and without price.

- Isaiah 55:1

Buying without money does not mean you should expect what you desire to simply materializes out of thin air! It is acquiring what you want through a *mental transaction.* Jesus said, *"Whatever you ask for in prayer, **believe that you receive it, then you will have it**" (Mark 11:24).*

"HOW CAN YOU RECEIVE SOMETHING BEFORE HAVING IT?"

The answer lies in your *imagination.* It is in your imagination that you first take receipt of the mental equivalent of what you desire. This is validated by *experiencing* the same emotion and gratitude for the mental equivalent as you would for its physical counterpart. When you truly believe that you have received what you ask for, you have completed the mental transaction.

As mentioned in the prologue, the only difference between receiving something mentally and having it physically is time. At the right time, the opportunity will come for you to *have* what you *received*. That opportunity can come in the form of money, a gift from someone, a massive discount in price, or a whole raft of other possibilities. To transliterate Jesus' words,

"Whoever has *(mental currency)* **will be given more** *(in their hands)*; **whoever does not have (mental currency), even what they have will be taken from them."** *(Mark 4:25)*

ABUNDANCE VS LACK AND LIMITATION

When you anchor your beliefs in the wisdom and infinite resources of the Kingdom, you can have whatever you desire *(Mark 11:24)*. You will not see the need to compete or take what belongs to someone else! On the other hand, a mind focused on materiality thinks in terms of lack and limitation. The paradigm of lack and limitation is *worldly* thinking - **a mind based on how things appear.** People who think this way feel the need to compete to *'get their piece of the pie,'* not realizing they can *create* their own pie! Due to the perceived notion of scarcity, they tend to believe that one person's wealth relates to another's person's poverty or another person's success is another person's failure. Many even believe that if someone is rich, they probably have *'ripped off'* the poor or working class! From this scarcity mentality, the idea of owning an expensive luxury item is considered wasteful and extravagant, and such items should be *'sold and given to the poor.'* However, like Jesus, a Kingdom-minded person sees no need to think like this because they know that:

• Nothing is wasted on them
• They are more valuable than any expensive luxury item
• Out of heaven's abundance, they can do good to the poor
  without the need to sell what they have.

There is only *one reason* why a rich person should sell all that they have and give to the poor, which I will discuss later.

Undoubtedly, one of the hallmarks of the Kingdom mindset is being a *cheerful* giver. No matter what their financial status is at the time, a Kingdom-minded person can give cheerfully to others, knowing that *there is more* where that came from. Sometimes, God requires us to give sacrificially, not to diminish what we have, but to *expand* our capacity for receiving much more. If, however, you are of the mind that *'things are scarce'*, then you are less likely to make such a sacrifice.

TRUTH V FACTS

The key to entering the Kingdom lies in the way you think. How you think will determine what you see, and what you see will determine what you experience. God wants you to have His mind - *the mind of Christ*, so you may see and experience life from Heaven's perspective. Where others saw lack and insufficiency, Jesus saw prosperity and abundance. Where others saw sickness and disease, Jesus saw health and well-being. When Lazarus died, Jesus said he was asleep! When you see and do things from Heaven's perspective, your everyday life will reflect the *truth* despite the facts. Spiritually speaking, truth and facts are not always the same.

• Facts are the reality of the physical outer world.
• Truth is the reality of the Spirit.
• Truth is eternal and unchangeable.
• Facts are temporal and can be changed.

Throughout His earthly ministry, Jesus demonstrated to thousands upon thousands how *facts* can be changed by *'truth.'* The facts killed Lazarus, but the truth brought him back to life. When 'truth' is put into action:

• The blind will receive their sight
• The lame will walk
• The lepers will be cleansed
• The deaf will hear and
• The dead will be raised!

These are just a fraction of heavenly realities that can be manifested on the earth. The truth, therefore, is **the power to change the facts.** God said, *"Let the weak say I am strong."* In other words,

'Let truth supersede the facts."

By that principle, we can also say, *"Let the sick say I am well"* or *"Let the poor say I am rich!"* No situation or circumstance in this earthly life is *'set in stone.'* The tangible realities of this physical world are malleable to the intangible reality of Heaven. We need only align our beliefs and thinking to 'truth.' We must, therefore, beware of the doctrine of the Pharisees and the Sadducees and not think according to outer appearances and materiality. The priorities of the world, that being:

- The lust of the eyes
- The lust of the flesh and
- The pride of life...

...are all based on how things appear.

> **The reason God does not want you to be so materialistic is to prevent you from becoming bankrupt!**

To reiterate, a mind framed by outer appearances and materiality thinks in terms of lack and limitation. That being the case, contrary to what we've been conditioned to believe, the reason why God does not want you to be so *'materialistic'* is to prevent you from becoming spiritually, emotionally, and financially bankrupt! **God wants you to be rich** - inwardly and outwardly! Through your union and communion with Him, in the confines of your heart, He wants to reward you openly, giving you exceeding, abundantly more than you ask or think *(Ephesians 3:20)*. However, that is impossible if your mind is set on materiality and keeping all that you have!

When you understand that **the Kingdom of God is within you** and that *'mind comes before matter,'* heaven's treasure will be open to you. No matter your financial status, God will meet your needs according to His riches in you, rather than the limited resources of your outer world. Ultimately, *you will prosper!*

CHAPTER 11

WHERE IS YOUR TREASURE?

---◆---

"Lay up for yourselves treasures in heaven,
where neither moth nor rust destroys"

 You can now imagine how frustrated Jesus must have been when His disciples misconstrued His warning about the doctrine of the Pharisees as a rebuke for forgetting to bring bread!

"Do you not yet understand or remember the five loaves of the five thousand and how many baskets you took up? Nor the seven loaves of the four thousand and how many large baskets you took up? How is it you do not understand that I did not speak to you concerning bread?"

- Mathew 16:9-11

Despite all the miracles they had witnessed, the disciples still thought in terms of lack and limitation. Worse still, by thinking Jesus was angry with them for not bringing bread, they obviously thought He had the same mindset *(which must have been quite an insult to Him)!* Unfortunately, Jesus is still misunderstood by those failing to interpret His words in the context of His overall message. No more so than when He told the Jews not to lay up for themselves treasures on the earth.

"Do not lay up for yourselves treasures on earth, where moth and rust destroy and where thieves break in and steal; but lay up for yourselves treasures in heaven, where neither moth nor rust destroys and where thieves do not break in and steal. For where your treasure is, there your heart will be also."

- Matthew 6:19-21

If we take a *literal* view of the above text, Jesus appears to be saying we should not have any material riches or earthly possessions laid up for ourselves. Indeed, that is the view many Christians subscribe to. However, when Jesus spoke of treasure, He was not talking about money, riches, or material possessions; He was talking about *the treasure of your heart.*

> *Your life is a perfect reflection of the state of your heart.*

*For every tree is known by its own fruit. For men do not gather figs from thorns, nor do they gather grapes from a bramble bush. A good man out of the **good treasure of his heart** brings forth good; and an evil man out of the **evil treasure of his heart** brings forth evil. For out of the abundance of the heart his mouth speaks.*

- Luke 6:44-45

Your heart *(also known as the subconscious mind)* is the center of your spiritual and physical life. It is the faculty that reflects the person you are, what you believe, and how you see yourself. Hence the well-known proverb:

'As he thinks in his heart, so is he.'
(Proverbs 23:7)

In the original Greek text, the word 'treasure' is the word *'thesauros.'* This is where the English word, *'Thesaurus,'* originates. Thesauros refers to a casket, receptacle, or storehouse in which precious valuables are kept. It is not the treasure itself but the place where treasure is kept.

"SO, WHAT IS THE 'TREASURE' YOUR HEART?"

The simple answer is **thought**. Thoughts are the seed of life. We live in a world intricately woven by the fibers of thought. Like any other seed, thoughts need soil to germinate in, and your heart is that soil.

According to Luke 6:45, there is *'Good treasure'* and *'Evil treasure'* of the heart. This could only refer to the type of thoughts you adhere to. If life seems to be going against you, it is the result of your heart being contaminated with *toxic thoughts*. If, however, you are winning in every sphere of life, it is because your heart is full of good or positive thoughts. What is most interesting is the fact that whether good or evil, toxic or positive, Jesus calls the thoughts of your heart *'treasure.'*

Not only is your heart the storehouse for your thoughts, it can also be home to **God's thoughts.** As a man or woman created in God's image, you have the potential to think like God! Just one thought from God - an idea, a flash of inspiration, can completely transform your life. God's thoughts are His reality. When you think like God, *His reality becomes your reality.* As a result, what is deemed impossible by others becomes *'very'* possible for you. Unfortunately, many believe it is not possible, or even sacrilegious to think like God and would be quick to quote from the book of Isaiah:

"For My thoughts are not your thoughts, nor are your ways My ways," says the Lord. "For as the heavens are higher than the earth, so are My ways higher than your ways, and My thoughts than your thoughts"

- Isaiah 55:8-9

However, God did not say this to *differentiate* Himself from us but instead underscore our fundamental problem. That being, **the depths to which our thoughts have fallen.** Jesus, who is the mind of God, said, *If you abide in Me, and My words abide in you, you will ask what you desire, and it shall be done for you. (John 15:7)*

To the degree that the word of God frames your thinking is to the degree to which you can manifest divine life. That is, in essence, the good news of the Kingdom. The spiritual terminology for a mind that is the storehouse for God's thoughts is *'Treasure in Heaven!'* Therefore, laying up treasure in heaven requires one to store God's word or thoughts *in their heart.* God said to Joshua,

This Book of the Law shall not depart from your mouth, but you shall meditate in it day and night, that you may observe to do according to all that is written in it. For then you will make your way prosperous, and then you will have good success.

- Joshua 1:8

God's thoughts are the *'incorruptible seed'* that can only produce *'good success.'* It is for this reason that Jesus wants us to lay up treasure in heaven. Your treasure in heaven manifests itself into all the good that God desires for you - divine health, prosperity, joy, peace, and success! Your treasure in heaven will make you rich on the earth!

"IF LAYING UP TREASURE IN HEAVEN ENABLES ONE TO BECOME MATERIALLY RICH, WHY DOES JESUS WARN US NOT TO LAY UP FOR OURSELVES TREASURES ON EARTH?"

Laying up treasures on earth refers to the mind that seeks *security* in the accumulation of earthly possessions. But as previously explained, this will only lead to *lack and limitation.* Jesus wants us to have the good that we desire. The only reason He gives to why we should not lay up treasure on earth is that it is *subject to theft or decay.*

> **You can lose riches, but you can never lose wealth!**

Therefore, His objection is not to us having material wealth; but losing it! **God wants you to have treasure you cannot lose!** The best way to achieve that is by laying up for yourself the treasure of God's thoughts in your heart.

There is a misconception that heavenly treasure is for the enjoyment of life *after* death. But that is not entirely true. Having treasure in heaven is first and foremost for the enjoyment of life *before* death. Eternal life is here and now, and God desires for you to live life abundantly in this world and in the world to come.

BEING RICH V BEING WEALTHY

Those who have treasure in heaven possess something far more valuable than any precious stone. They possess wealth! If you wish to live a prosperous life, you must aim to be wealthy, not just rich. Someone who is a millionaire may be rich but not necessarily wealthy. A rich person has an abundance of money and material possessions. A wealthy person, however, possesses the means to prosper no matter the circumstances. As mentioned earlier, Joseph was a prosperous man, even *as a slave!* That was because he had *inner wealth*. As a result, it was only a matter of time that the wealth inside him would manifest into the rich and powerful man he became.

If a wealthy person, peradventure, loses their money, they have the means to make it back again. On the other hand, if a rich person loses their money, they will most likely never regain what they lost. **You can lose riches, but you can never lose wealth!** Many stories abound, of those who win 10's or even 100's of millions of dollars in the lottery, only to quickly lose all that they won through excessive spending and poor financial decisions. Not only did they lose what they have, but tmany of them found themselves in more debt than they were in before, with their personal lives in complete disarray. They were rich but not wealthy.

So, the main difference between a rich person and a wealthy person is **sustainability**. While a rich person is highly susceptible to losing what they have, a wealthy person has amassed enough income-producing assets that they no longer have to worry about money. A wealthy person cultivates a way of life that maximizes the likelihood that they will be successful. Rather than dabbling in fruitless deeds like gambling, drugs, and other vices, they find ways to work smarter, freeing up their time to focus on things that matter most. Wealthy people focus on *long-term economic growth*. They are driven by purpose and passion, not greed. Most importantly, wealth gives you the freedom to spend your time *however you want*. Being rich, and living a luxurious lifestyle, may look like fun from the outside, but without wealth, such a lifestyle will be short-lived.

PUT YOUR TRUST IN GOD

The Bible often portrays the rich in a negative light, leading many to believe it is ungodly to be rich.

There is one who makes himself rich, yet has nothing; and one who makes himself poor, yet has great riches.

- Proverbs 13:7

God has put down the mighty from their thrones, and exalted the lowly. He has filled the hungry with good things, and the rich He has sent away empty.

- Luke 1:52-53

Woe to you who are rich, for you have received your consolation.

- Luke 6:24

Then Jesus said to His disciples, "Assuredly, I say to you that it is hard for a rich man to enter the kingdom of heaven. And again I say to you, it is easier for a camel to go through the eye of a needle than for a rich man to enter the kingdom of God."

- Matthew 19:23-24

However, it is important to understand that in many instances, when the Bible speaks of the rich, it is referring to those whose trust and security lies in the limited resources of their bank account rather than in the unlimited resources of the Kingdom.

The rich man's wealth is his strong city, and like a high wall in his own esteem.

- Proverbs 18:11

"Here is the man who did not make God his strength, But trusted in the abundance of his riches, And strengthened himself in his wickedness."

- Psalm 52:7

God wants you to prosper and have all the good that you desire. But having what you desire must be born from your trust in Him, putting mind before matter.

"Blessed is the man who trusts in the Lord, and whose hope is the Lord. For he shall be like a tree planted by the waters, which spreads out its roots by the river, and will not fear when heat comes; But its leaf will be green, and will not be anxious in the year of drought, nor will cease from yielding fruit."

- Jeremiah 17:7-8

When we manifest things from the spiritual realm into the physical world, they move from being eternal to being finite and temporal. This reveals the fallacy of putting one's trust in material things. As mentioned, material things are for our use and enjoyment, *not for our security*. **Our security lies in God, whose Kingdom is within us.** When your mind is full of the good treasure of God's thoughts, you can have the life that you desire.

CHAPTER 12

THE SPIRIT OF WISDOM

---◆---

"And thou shalt speak unto all that are wise hearted,
whom I have filled with the spirit of wisdom"

Wealth is a mindset, much the same as being poor is. Your mind is your greatest asset and, when put to good use, will cause you to prosper. That is why you must lay up for yourself, *'treasures in heaven'* - renewing your mind to the way God thinks. The wealth gained from God's thoughts is more valuable than silver, gold, or any other commodity. Even if it cost you all you had to obtain, you would still be far better off than the rich who are void of it. That is because true wealth is **wisdom.**

Happy is the man who finds wisdom, and the man who gains understanding; for her proceeds are better than the profits of silver, and her gain than fine gold. She is more precious than rubies, and all the things you may desire cannot compare with her. Length of days is in her right hand, In her left hand riches and honor. Her ways are ways of pleasantness, and all her paths are peace. She is a tree of life to those who take hold of her, and happy are all who retain her. The Lord by wisdom founded the earth; by understanding He established the heavens. By His knowledge the depths were broken up, and clouds drop down the dew.

- Proverbs 3:13-20

Wisdom is God's modus operandi. It is the means by which He created the world. By wisdom, kings reign, and princes decree justice. Even before he was endowed with divine wisdom, King Solomon was wise enough to ask God for wisdom rather than riches for himself. As a result, God gave him wealth, riches, and fame beyond any king before or after him *(2 Chronicles 1:9–12)*.

Not only will wisdom make you wealthy, but it will also guide your life. It will give you discernment and help you make the right decisions, especially in your dealings with others. Indeed, you are not wealthy if you cannot forge successful relationships with others, especially those who can open doors for you. That could well be why Jesus endorses the use of *unrighteous mammon* to make friends!

Wisdom also enables you to achieve your life goals faster by working smart rather than working hard. Hence the proverb:

"If the ax is dull, and one does not sharpen the edge, then he must use more strength; but wisdom brings success."

- Ecclesiastes 10:10

TRUE WISDOM

Our idea of wisdom should not be limited to sound judgment or intellectual knowledge. WISDOM IS SUPERNATURAL. The ancient Hebrews understood this truth. That is why they linked the miraculous works of Jesus to wisdom.

And when the Sabbath had come, He began to teach in the synagogue. And many hearing Him were astonished, saying, **"Where did this Man get these things? And what wisdom is this which is given to Him, that such mighty works are performed by His hands!"**

- Mark 6:2

All the miracles of the Bible were an expression of wisdom, whether performed by Jesus, Moses, Elijah, or Elisha. Even the Magi were called *'Wise men'* because they understood the spiritual nature of wisdom.

SO, WHAT IS TRUE WISDOM?

To find the answer, let us again use the law of first mention.

Wisdom first appears in the Bible when God told Moses to speak to the *wise-hearted*.

"And thou shalt speak unto all that are wise hearted, whom I have filled with the spirit of wisdom, that they may make Aaron's garments to consecrate him, that he may minister unto me in the priest's office."

- Exodus 28:3 KJV

The people described as *'wise hearted'* in scripture are the artisans. As previously explained, artisans are highly talented individuals with particular creative skills such as painting, embroidery, engraving, carpentry, and other creative work. However, their essential skill lies in their ability to manifest what they see with their imagination. Once an image is formed in their minds, they materialize it through the skillful application of knowledge and understanding. It was this ability that made the artisans so essential to Moses. Not just because of their creativity but also their ability to manifest his God-given vision. Like all visionaries, Moses was tasked with the responsibility of materializing on earth what exists in heaven. In this case, it was the tabernacle.

*...there are priests who offer the gifts according to the law; who serve the copy and shadow of the heavenly things, as Moses was divinely instructed when he was about to make the tabernacle. For He [God] said, **"See that you make all things according to the pattern shown you on the mountain."***

- Hebrews 8:4-5

It was of vital importance that the tabernacle be reproduced exactly as seen. That's because everything about the tabernacle had a symbolic meaning. The furnishings, the fabrics, the colors, even the wooden pegs were of great symbolic value. That is why Moses shared his vision with individuals God had given a spirit of wisdom. Individuals spiritually endowed to capture his vision. God left nothing to chance! He filled Bezaleel and Aholiab with the Spirit of wisdom to do artistic designs using gold, silver, and bronze, cut jewels for setting, and fashion intricate wood carvings. All the furnishings and regalia for the tabernacle, including:

• The tabernacle of meeting,

• The ark of the Testimony,

• The mercy seat that is on it,

• The furniture of the tabernacle,

• The table and its utensils,

• The pure gold lampstand with all its utensils,

• The altar of incense,

• The altar of burnt offering with all its utensils,

• The laver and its base,

• The garments of ministry,

• The holy garments for Aaron the priest
  and the garments for his sons,

were all created by artisans anointed with the Spirit of wisdom. Even the women who spun yarns of goats hair with their hands were stirred in their hearts with wisdom *(Exodus 31 and 35)*.

RECOGNIZE WHAT YOU HAVE

Therefore, wisdom encompasses the creative process required to manifest ideas, images, and concepts formed or captured in the mind. It is how thought becomes matter, the unseen becomes seen, and the intangible becomes tangible. Sound judgment, righteousness, and the quality of being wise all stem from the spiritual principles of manifesting what is first seen in the mind.

> *Everything that you experience in life is a result of what you saw or did not see!*

The Spirit of Wisdom is the supernatural enablement to see with greater clarity into the spiritual realm. Usually accompanied by knowledge and understanding, the Spirit of wisdom opens your eyes to solutions, possibilities, and opportunities you would not have otherwise seen. Everything that you experience in life is a result of what you saw or did not see! Jeremiah alluded to this when he said of the man who *'makes flesh his strength'* - trusting in materiality and external things rather than what God reveals to his mind,

*"He shall be like a shrub in the desert, **and shall not see when good comes,** but shall inhabit the parched places in the wilderness, in a salt land which is not inhabited."*

- Jeremiah 17:6

If you currently feel like you're in a dry land, void of resources and opportunities, while others around you are flourishing, it could well be that you did not see when *'good'* came, or even when you had it! Jesus said at various times,

"Whoever has, to him more will be given, and he will have abundance; but whoever does not have, even what he has will be taken away from him."

- Matthew 13:12

HOW CAN SOMETHING BE TAKEN AWAY FROM YOU THAT YOU DON'T HAVE?

This can only happen when you fail to see or recognize what you already have, not just in physical life but fundamentally in your mind. John said,

"This is the confidence that we have in Him, that if we ask anything according to His will, He hears us. And if we know that He hears us, whatever we ask, we know that we have the petitions that we have asked of Him."

- 1 John 5:14-15

Simply put, whatever you ask God for, *according to His will*, is yours. If you believe it is yours *(spiritually)*, then you will have it physically. That is the abundance that you will receive. If, however, you overlook, or fail to recognize what God has made yours, then it will be taken away. Therefore, much of what you may believe to be unanswered prayer is the failure to recognize what was already yours. The fact that Jesus states this principle on numerous occasions points to how vitally important it is to recognize what you have.

"People only give up on their dreams
when they feel they do not have the opportunity to fulfill them.
However, it is not the absence of opportunities that is the
problem, but instead, the failure to recognize opportunities
and resources embedded in their lives."

THE POWER OF VISION

The Spirit of wisdom, therefore, is *the power of vision*. A fundamental part of living is missed when you underestimate what is revealed in your mind. VISION IS THE BLUEPRINT FOR YOUR LIFE. It is your inner GPS that will guide you to your destiny. It controls your choices, routines, focus, career, relationships, and ultimately how you spend your precious time. When you have a clear, compelling vision, life becomes simple; because once you know what you must achieve, you automatically know *what not to do*. Vision, therefore, unlocks your entire life!

Many major breakthroughs, like our understanding of the structure of molecules, the periodic table of elements, and a host of other world-changing discoveries, resulted from what was seen in dreams and visions. The course of history has been forged by those who learned to put their trust in what was revealed in their minds.

General George Patton, one of the most successful generals in history, had so many dreams about strategy and his enemies' plans that his personal secretary became very accustomed to getting calls from him in the middle of the night with instructions he had received in his dreams. Overall, General Patton placed more trust in his dreams than the intelligence he received from his officers on the ground.

Harriet Tubman, a former slave who led hundreds of slaves to freedom through the underground railroad, said she regularly dreamed about where to go to find safe houses. She never lost a single *passenger.*

CONVERTING WHAT YOU SEE
TO WHAT YOU NEED

That being said, it is not enough to see solutions in dreams and visions; you must also *materialize what you see!* A person who has vision but does not materialize what they see is just a dreamer - Not a visionary! As well as enabling you to see visions and dreams with greater clarity, the Spirit of Wisdom also empowers you to convert what you see to what you or others need. Converting what you see in your mind to what millions of others need or want is the key to high achievement. This one action alone will inevitably make you very successful. Larry Page became a Billionaire because he had the wisdom to convert what he saw in his dream into Google, ushering in an age where we all have knowledge at our fingertips.

To reiterate, people only give up on their dreams when they feel they do not have the resources or the opportunity to fulfill them. But that is only because they do not recognize the power of their mind. As long as your mind is intact, you have what you need to set in motion all that is necessary to change your life and fulfill your dreams.

CHAPTER 13

MANIFESTING THE FATHER

◆

The Son can do nothing of Himself,
but what He sees the Father do

The value of your imagination is more than you can perceive. Even great scientific minds like Albert Einstein referred to imagination as *'The preview of life's coming attractions.'* When your imagination is anointed with the Spirit of Wisdom, you can accomplish miraculous things. This certainly was the case with

Jesus, who, according to Isaiah, had the Spirit of Wisdom, and as a result, was able to *see* what the Father was doing.

Then Jesus answered and said to them, "Most assuredly, I say to you, the Son can do nothing of Himself, but what He sees the Father do; for whatever He does, the Son also does in like manner."

- John 5:19

Jesus' ability to *see the Father* was not by divine visitation, a burning bush, or any of the spectacular manifestations displayed in the old testament. The Father was whom He saw in His mind. **Jesus was obedient to whom He saw in His mind!** All the miraculous things He did, emanated from what He saw His Father doing on the screen of His imagination. His entire life, in the physical world, was about *manifesting the Father.*

What infuriated the Jews so much was Jesus' declaration that He was *'One with the Father,'* a statement punishable by death *(John 10:30-33)!* However, Jesus was never fearful about proclaiming His union with the Father, despite the number of times He was nearly stoned because of it. He made it clear that,

• When you see the Son, you see the Father.
• You cannot see the Father unless you see the Son.
• You cannot know the Father unless you know the Son.
• Only the Son can reveal the Father.

The Son, therefore, is the reflection of the Father, manifesting His life, character, and power. That is the fundamental reason why **Jesus**

could not have been poor or live a life of poverty because *that is not the life of Father!* Even in the parables Jesus told, the Father is often portrayed as a wealthy landowner. The only time Jesus became poor was *on the cross*, where He became sin for our redemption. That in itself required a momentary separation from the Father, evidenced by the loud cry, *"Eloi, Eloi, lama sabachthani?"* which is translated, *"My God, My God, why have You forsaken Me?"*

WHO DO YOU THINK YOU ARE?

If the Father can only be seen through the Son, then the person Jesus recognized as the Father could only have appeared as Himself! Thus, what Jesus saw the Father doing in the imagination of His heart, was what He saw *Himself* doing. However, in seeing Himself, He understood that He was really seeing the Father. Therefore, the mighty works Jesus did, emanated from His own *self-image*. In like manner, your life is a reflection of your self-image - the person you see yourself to be in the mirror of your heart.

As in water, face reflects face, so a man's
heart reveals the man.
- Proverbs 27:19

As he thinks in his heart, so is he.
- Proverbs 23:7

Keep your heart with all diligence,
*for out of it spring **the issues of life**.*
- Proverbs 4:23

> **If your self-concept is anything other than Christ, then you have missed the mark!**

The *'issues of life'* that springs from your heart are *a reflection* of whom you see yourself to be. Even the events that took place in your life that seemed to be beyond your control were the product of your own self-image. If you looked at your reflection in a mirror and saw a speck on your face, you would not attempt to remove the speck by wiping the mirror! What's in the mirror is merely a reflection. The reality is what stands before the mirror. In like manner, your outer world is a reflection of your own self-image. Rather than trying to change things outwardly, you can exert an incredible amount of control over your life and the things you attract by **determining your self-image**. In the field of personal development, life coaches, motivational speakers, and the like, will encourage you to adopt a positive self-image and strive to be the best version of yourself. Although that is a step in the right direction, when God said, *"Let Us make man in our image,"* Christ was whom He had in mind.

CHRIST IS THE ULTIMATE YOU!

His ministry on earth was but a demonstration of **who you really are**. That is why He said, *"Most assuredly, I say to you, he who believes in Me, the works that I do he will do also; and greater works than these he will do, because I go to My Father" (John 14:2)*. Although you have the ability to form your own self-image, if your self-concept is anything other than Christ, then you have *'missed the mark,'* falling short of the glory of God! As Paul explains, **God has reconciled humanity to Himself, through Christ** *(Romans 5:10)*. It is only for humanity to realize this truth! Jesus described this reconciliation with the Father as:

"I am in my Father, you are in me, and I am in you." (John 14:20).

Oneness with Christ brings you into oneness with the Father. Therefore, when you identify with Christ *(embracing His Spirit)*, you embrace your divine identity as a Son of God!

*But he that is joined unto the Lord is **one spirit.***

- 1 Corinthians 6:17

*For you are all **sons of God** through faith in Christ Jesus.*

- Galatians 3:26

*For as many as are led by the Spirit of God, these are **sons of God.***

- Romans 8:14

*Behold what manner of love the Father has bestowed on us, that we should be called **sons of God**! Therefore, the world does not know us, because it did not know Him.*

- 1 John 3:1

*Beloved, now are we the **sons of God**, and it does not yet appear what we shall be: but we know that, when he shall appear, we shall be like him; for we shall see him as he is.*

- 1 John 3:2

ONE WITH THE FATHER

'Son of God' is a *genderless* term that transcends the traditional Parent-child concept. To be a Son of God means you *recognize* God as your Father, and more importantly, God recognizes you as His Son. Although many may call God their Father as a term of endearment, the ancient Jews understood that when someone calls God their Father, they make themselves *equal with God*.

*But Jesus answered them, "My Father has been working until now, and I have been working." Therefore, the Jews sought all the more to kill Him, because He not only broke the Sabbath, but also said that **God was His Father, making Himself equal with God.***

- John 5:17-18

What the Jews saw as blasphemy was, in fact, divine identity. To be a Son of God is to be equal with God because the Father and Son are one. It is only sinful to believe you are equal with God if you see yourself as *separate* from God. Seeing oneself as separate from God is the fundamental flaw in man's thinking and self-image. That is why Paul urges us to adopted the Christ mindset:

Let this mind be in you which was also in Christ Jesus, *who, being in the form of God, **did not consider it robbery to be equal with God,** but made Himself of no reputation, taking the form of a bondservant, and coming in the likeness of men.*

- Philippians 2:5-7

On a subconscious level, your self-image reflects your perception of God. That is why your outer world is so malleable to the way you think. Unfortunately, many people suffer from a poor self-image, and the image of God in us is distorted, fractured, and broken! As a result, many people live broken lives in a broken society.

Thankfully, God has paved the way for the shattered pieces of His image in us to be restored through Christ, who is the *complete picture* of our ultimate selves.

For whom He foreknew, He also predestined to be conformed to the image of His Son, that He might be the firstborn among many brethren.

- Romans 8:29

He Himself gave some to be apostles, some prophets, some evangelists, and some pastors and teachers, for the equipping of the saints for the work of ministry, for the edifying of the body of Christ, ***till we all come to the unity of the faith and of the knowledge of the Son of God, to a perfect man, to the measure of the stature of the fullness of Christ.***

- Ephesians 4:11-13

WHAT DO YOU SEE YOURSELF DOING?

As a Son of God, you must also manifest the Father, for God has called us to be *unique* expressions of Himself. To do this, you must also *see* what the Father is doing. The question is,

"WHAT GREAT THING DO YOU SEE YOURSELF DOING?"

Because the great things you see yourself achieving in life, is in fact, what the Father is doing! Like Jesus, you must recognize that the person that looks like you in a God-given vision is the Father at work.

As mentioned, you are called to be a unique expression of the Father. As such, you must know who God is, in you, and *as you*, rather than trying to emulate someone else's perception and expression of the Father. Your expression of the Father may be as a CEO of a global company, an award-winning Actor or Actress, a best-selling Author, a groundbreaking Inventor, a Billionaire Philanthropist, the Prime Minister, a Fashion Designer, a Publisher, a Michelin Chef, an Architect, Nurse, Craftsman, Teacher, and all the wonderful professions that serve to improve and transform our lives.

•

Don't be afraid to step out to achieve your big dream,
because it is what the Father is doing in and as you.

•

Be obedient to the passion, vision,
and desire God has placed in
your heart, and what you see yourself
achieving in your mind.

•

Never let the opinions of others
stifle your dream.

CHAPTER 14

THE LESSON FOR THE RICH YOUNG RULER

PART TWO

---◆---

"Blessed is the man who trusts in the Lord,
and whose hope is the Lord"

onsidering all that has been said in the previous chapters, you may now look at the rich young ruler's encounter with Jesus from a different perspective than the purveyors of the virtues of poverty. Here's a reminder of that encounter:

Now as He was going out on the road, one came running, knelt before Him, and asked Him, "Good Teacher, what shall I do that I may inherit eternal life?" So Jesus said to him, "Why do you call Me good? No one is good but One, that is, God. You know the commandments: 'Do not commit adultery,' 'Do not murder,' 'Do not steal,' 'Do not bear false witness,' 'Do not defraud,' 'Honor your father and your mother.'

"And he answered and said to Him, "Teacher, all these things I have kept from my youth." Then Jesus, looking at him, loved him, and said to him,

*"One thing you lack: **Go your way, sell whatever you have and give to the poor, and you will have treasure in heaven; and come, take up the cross, and follow Me."***

But he was sad at this word, and went away sorrowful, for he had great possessions. *Then Jesus looked around and said to His disciples, **"How hard it is for those who have riches to enter the kingdom of God!"***

- Mark 10:17-22

The question is,

"CAN YOU HONESTLY STILL BELIEVE THAT WHEN JESUS INSTRUCTED THE RICH YOUNG RULER TO...

- SELL WHAT HE HAD
- GIVE IT TO THE POOR,
- HAVE TREASURE IN HEAVEN,

- TAKE UP HIS CROSS AND FOLLOW HIM,

...HE WAS INVITING HIM TO LIVE OUT THE REST OF HIS LIFE IN POVERTY?"

I assure you, *that was not the case.* As a matter of fact, the instructions given to the rich young ruler *(what many believe to be irrefutable proof that believers are not supposed to be rich)*, was in fact, **an opportunity for him to have far more than he had before.**

I can say this with confidence because it is not the nature of God to ask so much of anyone and not give them more *in this lifetime.* Jesus assures us that,

"No one who has left house or brothers or sisters or father or mother or wife or children or lands, for My sake and the gospel's, who shall not receive a hundredfold now in this time - houses and brothers and sisters and mothers and children and lands, with persecutions - and in the age to come, eternal life."

- Mark 10:29-30

It is impossible to out-give the God who exalts the humble and will not even hear your prayer unless you first believe **He is a rewarder of those who seek Him.** God is a kind and generous Father, seeking any opportunity to bless His children *lavishly.* But, unfortunately, like the wicked and lazy servant in the parable of the talents, many religion folk see Him as an *austere* man, *reaping where He did not sow and gathering where He scattered no seed (Luke 19:21).* As a result, they are quick to accept the most draconian beliefs about His will.

Had the rich young ruler taken the opportunity to be mentored by the *'Author of Life,'* under His tutelage he would have:

- Learned the secrets of his true identity,
- Learned the divine laws of the mind and how to manifest the good that he desires.
- Learned how to convert what he sees [with his mind] to what he needs [in his hands].
- Learned how to use the power of his tongue to change the facts with the truth.
- Learned to live a life of vision.

Ultimately, he would have learned how to **manifest the Father!**

You may ask,

"WHY THEN DID JESUS TELL THE RICH YOUNG RULER TO SELL WHAT HE HAD AND GIVE TO THE POOR?"

First and foremost, when Jesus gave the young man that particular instruction, He did so, out of love! He was not trying to *'trip him up'* so He could prove how greedy rich people are! Neither was He trying to disprove that he was not perfect concerning the law. Indeed, when Jesus looked at him, *summing him up*, He concluded that there was only *'One thing'* that he lacked. How, many of us can honestly say that Jesus would only find *one thing* lacking in us? The young man was as sincere as he could be but lacked one thing, that being - *total trust in God!*

TRUST IN GOD

Blessed is the man who trusts in the Lord, and whose hope is the Lord. For he shall be like a tree planted by the waters, which spreads out its roots by the river, and will not fear when heat comes; But its leaf will be green, and will not be anxious in the year of drought, nor will cease from yielding fruit.

- Jeremiah 17:7-8

Trusting God is the hallmark of spirituality, the beginning of wisdom, and the key to successful living. Only through trust in God can one rise above the turbulence of physical life. Indeed, the person who trusts in God can expect to be *fruitful* in all seasons! In the same way, Jesus was able to sleep peacefully on a boat in the midst of a storm, when you trust in God, you too can be at peace even in the face of surmounting adversity.

As demonstrated by Elisha, trusting in God opens your eyes to the fact that there are more who are with you than against you *(spiritually and physically)* and that you can rely on the unlimited resources of the Kingdom *within* to come to your aid, and meet your needs.

When the servant of the man of God arose early and went out, there was an army, surrounding the city with horses and chariots. And his servant said to him,

"Alas, my master! What shall we do?" So he answered, "Do not fear, for those who are with us are more than those who are with them."

And Elisha prayed, and said, "Lord, I pray, open his eyes that he may see." Then the Lord opened the eyes of the young man, and he saw. And behold, the mountain was full of horses and chariots of fire all around Elisha. -

2 Kings 6:15-17

Ultimately, trust in God is the *master key* to manifestation, for when you have confidence in God, you have the assurance that what you ask for is already granted!

Now, this is the confidence that we have in Him, that if we ask anything according to His will, He hears us. And if we know that He hears us, whatever we ask, we know that we have the petitions that we have asked of Him.

-1 John 5:14-15

You can have anything you ask for according to His will, just by knowing that *God has heard you!* That is the level of trust God wants you to have in Him. Take some time to think about this profound truth because that alone will transform your life.

ETERNAL LIFE

Trust in God is what makes your mind fertile for treasure in heaven! As explained, treasure in heaven exemplifies the mind that has been renewed to the *word of God*. When your mind is renewed to the way God thinks, you can have what you desire! To think like God is to be like God, and to be like God is to *live like God*, and to live like God is to live as Christ. The life of Christ is **eternal life**, the very life God has embedded in our hearts.

He has made everything beautiful in its time. He has also set eternity in the human heart; yet no one can fathom what God has done from beginning to end.

- Ecclesiastes 3:11

'And this is eternal life, that they may know You, the only true God, and Jesus Christ whom You have sent.'

- John 17:3

Christ is the embodiment and ultimate expression of eternal life. Therefore, to inherit eternal life is to inherit Him. That is why, to the dismay of His would-be followers, He said, *"Whoever eats My flesh and drinks My blood has eternal life, and I will raise him up at the last day"* *(John 6:54).*

Although the *literal* interpretation of this statement caused many of His disciples to leave Him, it was the only way He could express the fact that *'He is Eternal life!'*

Therefore, what Jesus offered to the rich young ruler, was the very thing he was asking for, the opportunity to inherit eternal life by living *His* life. Not a life of lack and scarcity, but one of joy, peace, success, health, and wealth.

A DIRECT PATH

Jesus wanted the young man to have what he asked for but saw that his efforts to keep the law did nothing to renew his mind to divine thinking! He had treasure on earth *but none in heaven!* As a result, he placed his trust and security in riches, cutting himself off from the *'true riches'* God had in store for him. To that end, Jesus gave the young man a direct path to having treasure in heaven so he could manifest the life he desired. This was the path by which the young man could make the *paradigm shift* from trust in riches to total trust in God. The transition from self-reliance to God reliance. The change from working with his hands to *working with his mind!*

All he was required to do was,

"Sell whatever he had and give to the poor."

The only reason why Christ would require anyone to sell all they had and give to the poor is so they can have what they desire through trust in God!

THE ROLE OF RICH BELIEVERS

Jesus did not tell the young man to sell what he had because he was rich! It was purely because he placed his trust in material wealth. When He said, *"How hard it is for those who have riches to enter the kingdom of God!"* he clarified that statement by saying, *"How hard it is for those who **trust in riches** to enter the kingdom of God!"*

As often mentioned, God wants you to have money without money having you! This sentiment is reflected in this command *explicitly* made to those who are rich.

*Tell people who are rich **at this time** not to become egotistical and not to place their hope on their finances, which are uncertain. Instead, they need to hope in God, **who richly provides everything for our enjoyment.** Tell them to do good, to be rich in the good things they do, to be generous, and to share with others.*

-1 Timothy 6:17-18 CEB

Although the above command could apply to *all* who are rich, it applies explicitly to *rich believers*! For it is wealthy believers, in particular, God expects to be generous in helping others and finance the work of the gospel - *and indeed they did!* As mentioned in chapter 5, it was wealthy landowning believers who sold pieces of land and properties so that no one in the growing community of believers would be in lack or need. They also opened their homes to provide a haven for the early church. Homes large enough for many believers to gather together, break bread, and hear the word of God. It was in such a house that a young man named Eutychus fell from a *third-story* window while Paul was preaching. Such was the size of the homes they worshipped in (Acts 20:9).

Contrary to the belief that Christians should be *'poor on earth and rich in heaven,'* God is talking to believers who are rich *at this time.* In other words, He expects there to be believers who are *rich now,* not in heaven, nor in the world to come.

It should also be noted that at no point does God tell wealthy believers to sell all their worldly possessions to avoid the temptation of putting their trust in uncertain riches. On the contrary, if a wealthy believer maintains their trust in Him, He will continue to *richly provide* everything for their enjoyment!

Not all rich people place their trust in riches. On the flip side, not all those with low to moderate-income place their trust in God. Therefore, selling all your worldly goods or not owning lands or properties is not a blanket requirement that all must adhere to.

Through a personal relationship with God, you must follow the Holy Spirit's leading to do what is best to cultivate total trust in God and express eternal life. For the rich young ruler, selling what he had, and giving it to the poor, was what Jesus required him to do to develop his trust in God. Had he done so, the young man could have gained so much more than he sold, spiritually and materially.

CHAPTER 15

TAKE UP YOUR CROSS

"If anyone desires to come after Me, let him deny himself,
and take up his cross daily, and follow Me"

In stark contrast to the life of poverty promoted by various religious orders, Jesus gave the rich young ruler an opportunity to *be more*, and if he so wish, *have more* than he ever had before. You may ask,

"WHAT ABOUT THE COMMAND TO TAKE UP THE CROSS? DOES THAT NOT REQUIRE THOSE WHO FOLLOW CHRIST TO DIE-TO-SELF, WORLDLY AMBITIONS, AND MATERIAL WEALTH?"

After all,

"WHAT SHALL IT PROFIT A MAN, IF HE SHALL GAIN THE WHOLE WORLD, AND LOSE HIS OWN SOUL?" (MARK 8:36)

As the cross was an instrument of death, numerous commentators interpret taking up your cross as *death-to-self*. Based on this viewpoint, many in the church live a self-effacing life of sacrifice and unnecessary hardships, even to the point of losing friends and family. There are even those who scorn the idea of health, wealth, and prosperity, believing that we are simply called to **die** in this life so that we can reap an eternal reward in the hereafter! The scripture often quoted to support this view is,

"If anyone desires to come after Me, let him deny himself, and take up his cross daily, and follow Me. For whoever desires to save his life will lose it, but whoever loses his life for My sake will save it."

- Luke 9:23-24

As taught earlier, if we are to understand the word of God and divine thinking, we must first seek the inner, spiritual meaning of the word, rather than its outer, literal meaning. In principle, we must put *mind before matter!* When you adhere to literal meanings, you risk living a very draconian and disempowered life. That is why Paul said,

"The letter kills, but the Spirit gives life"

- 2 Corinthians 3:6.

The good news is that a believer's life need not be so harsh and emaciated, especially as the central theme of Jesus' teaching is that you can have the good that you desire *(health, wealth, peace, joy, success, and prosperity)* through the Kingdom of God in you!

Seek first the kingdom of God and His righteousness, **and all these things shall be added to you.**

- Matthew 6:33

LIFE AFTER DEATH

Although the cross was an instrument of death, it was also the path to resurrection and newness of life. From this perspective, rather than death-to-self, the cross represents *life after death*. When we read Matthew's rendering of *'taking up the cross,'* we get this same sense of life after death.

"If anyone desires to come after Me, let him deny himself, and take up his cross, and follow Me. For whoever desires to save his life will lose it, but whoever loses his life for My sake **will find it.***"*

- Matthew 16:24-25

Paul adds to this sentiment in his profound description of the born-again experience:

I have been crucified with Christ; **it is no longer I who live, but Christ lives in me;** *and the life which I now live in the flesh I live by faith in the Son of God, who loved me and gave Himself for me.*

- Galatians 2:20

For the born-again believer, it is Christ that lives! As a believer you are one with Him, manifesting *His life* as a Son of God.

Therefore, taking up one's cross is the putting to death of the:

• Negative self-image,

• Low self-worth,

• False identity

• and the distorted perception of God,

instilled in you from the day you were born. **That is the only death God requires of you.** But after death, there is resurrection and newness of life in Christ - your divine identity.

Paul puts it this way,

"Put off, concerning your former conduct, the old man which grows corrupt according to the deceitful lusts, and be renewed in the spirit of your mind, and that you put on the new man which was created according to God, in true righteousness and holiness."

- Ephesians 4:21-22)

It is the *'Old man'* that must die! The old man is the mind that:

- sees itself as separate from God.
- sees itself as the tail and not the head.
- sees itself as beneath and not above.
- is contaminated by the leaven of the Pharisees.

Overall, the old man is the mind trapped in the confines of physical life, lack and limitation, and external circumstances.

The *'New Man'* is the God identity expressed by the mind of Christ and a divine self-image. Embracing your divine self-image is the key to having whatever you want, spiritually or materially.

When Jesus said, *"What shall it profit a man if he shall gain the whole world and lose his own soul?"* He was not saying that you have to choose between the world or your soul. Instead, you must *prioritize* your soul over the world. You must *seek first the Kingdom*, put mind before matter, and address the issue of your divine identity. In so doing, *all things* will be added to you, **for all things are yours!**

*Therefore, let no man glory in men. **For all things are yours; Whether Paul, or Apollos, or Cephas, or the world, or life, or death, or things present, or things to come; all are yours; and ye are Christ's; and Christ is God's.***

- 1 Corinthians 3:21-23

BOOK 3

GOOD SUCCESS

WHAT IS SUCCESS?

S uccess means many things to many people. The oxford dictionary defines it as the accomplishment of an aim or purpose. Success guru, Earl Nightingale defined success as,

- *The successive realization of a worthy ideal.*

For many years, my personal definition of success was,

- *Achieving your goals without compromising your values.*

As good as these definitions may be,

- Where do your goals come from?
- Whose ideals are you trying to accomplish?

And most importantly,

• How do you determine your purpose?

If you struggle to answer these questions with confidence, then you are in danger of spending years trying to achieve goals that, when accomplished, leaves you:

Disappointed,
Dissatisfied,
Discontented,
and Unhappy!

Many have spent their whole career living by someone else's definition of success, or in many cases, *following the follower!* Not wanting to be caught up in this endless cycle, I turned to the Word of God to find a biblical definition for success. Interestingly, the word 'Success' only occurs once in the Bible, in the book of Joshua.

"This Book of the Law shall not depart from your mouth, but you shall meditate in it day and night, that you may observe to do according to all that is written in it. For then you will make your way prosperous, and then you will have good success."
- Joshua 1:8

Not only does the Bible say you can have success, but good success - success that is in alignment with God's word. The Hebrew word for success is *'Sakal,'* and although success only occurs *once* in the Bible, Sakal is used in various places throughout the scriptures under different translations. So I decided to study all the uses of Sakal in the Bible, and in so doing, discovered a more conclusive definition for success. This definition is one that you probably have not heard before and is framed by the three words used for Sakal:

- Guided.
- Knowledge.
- Identity.

Good success is the result of being,

'Guided by the Knowledge of Who You Are.'

Not the misguided identities we tend to label ourselves with, but your *divine identity* - the very image of God. When you look at the lives of some of God's leading servants, you will see that they owe their success to being guided by the knowledge of who they were. They all received a revelation of their true identity that defined the course of their lives.

Gideon, who first saw himself as the least in his father's house, received the revelation of being a *'Mighty Man of Valor.'* Abraham held onto the promise of being the *'Father of many nations,'* even when he was advanced in age. Once these men embraced their God-given identity, they were guided along their own pathway of victory, prosperity, and success.

So, success is really about **manifesting your identity,** and you only have good success when you express your true identity, your God-given identity, or what I call - THE ULTIMATE YOU.

WHY DO I SAY THE ULTIMATE YOU?

Because anyone who embraces their God-given identity can expect two things:

1. To live beyond ordinary human limitations
2. To achieve what others, deem impossible

God desires for you to embrace and express your *Ultimate Self.* To live an extraordinary life of success, power and abundance. This is the *Christ life!* The life you are promised, when you allow Christ **to be Himself in you.**

CHAPTER 16

MILK AND HONEY

"The Spirit of the Lord is upon Me, because He has anointed Me to preach the gospel to the poor"

Whether you agree or not, prosperity is the greatest incentive for much of what we do. Whether business, personal, or even charitable endeavors, success and prosperity are the underlying incentive. Unfortunately, words like *success and prosperity* are greeted with mixed reactions, especially within the Church. Worse still is the term *'prosperity gospel,'* which evokes images of the sheep being *fleeced* by the shepherd! However, apart from its financial aspect, prosperity encompasses advancement, progress, and succeeding in one's goals and purpose. When prosperity is mentioned in the Bible, it is often accompanied by the word *peace*. The Hebrew word for peace is *shalom*, which speaks of wholeness and completeness, with *nothing missing and nothing broken*. Shalom also encompasses health, security, success, happiness, wellness, and prosperity. Most importantly, shalom is the quintessential hallmark of God's presence - *the peace that passes all understanding.*

True prosperity, therefore, is an expression of God's presence. The Bible has many examples of individuals who prospered because God was *with* them. Joseph is the prime example used in this book.

*The Lord was with Joseph, and he was a successful man; and he was in the house of his master the Egyptian. **And his master saw that the Lord was with him and that the Lord made all he did to prosper in his hand.***

- Genesis 39:2-3

Prosperity is also what is promised to those who meditate and take delight in God's Word.

Blessed is the man who walks not in the counsel of the ungodly, nor stands in the path of sinners, nor sits in the seat of the scornful; but his delight is in the law of the Lord, and in His law, he meditates day and night. He shall be like a tree planted by the rivers of water, that brings forth its fruit in its season, whose leaf also shall not wither;

and whatever he does shall prosper.

- Psalm 1:1-3

This Book of the Law shall not depart from your mouth, but you shall meditate in it day and night, that you may observe to do according to all that is written in it. For then you will make your way prosperous, and then you will have good success.

- Joshua 1:8

It is, therefore, vital that you develop a positive attitude towards prosperity and all that comes with it. Not only is it central to the Abrahamic Covenant, it is also an integral part of the gospel - *if not the gospel itself!*

No doubt, many would strongly disagree with this, mainly because the gospel preached for the past millennia centers around being saved from hell and having life after death. Indeed, when Christians speak of being *'saved,'* that is just what they mean! However, as I will explain later in this book, your salvation requires you to *manifest the good you desire*, right here, right now, *in this lifetime*. As a matter of fact,

"IF YOU ARE NOT MANIFESTING THE GOOD YOU DESIRE, YOU ARE NOT A DISCIPLE OF CHRIST!"

Unfortunately, many in the church fail to attain the good they desire, or worse still, have such desires preached right out of them!

THE GOSPEL

In the book of Hebrews, the writer makes a profound parallel between the gospel that was preached by the early church and the gospel preached to the children of Israel as slaves in Egypt.

For indeed the gospel was preached to us as well as to them [the Hebrew slaves]; but the word which they heard did not profit them, not being mixed with faith in those who heard it.

- Hebrews 4:2

By making this parallel, the Spirit of God reveals that what was considered *'the gospel'* by the early church was, in essence, the same gospel preached to the children of Israel during their captivity in Egypt. Therefore, the gospel is by no means a new testament concept but an old testament promise. Moreover, it was a gospel preached to those who were *impoverished and enslaved.* A message that gave hope to a generation of people living in a system of *economic bondage.* That is why Jesus and His disciples preached the gospel to the poor.

*The Spirit of the Lord is upon Me, because **He has anointed Me to preach the gospel to the poor;** He has sent Me to heal the brokenhearted, to proclaim liberty to the captives and recovery of sight to the blind, to set at liberty those who are oppressed.*

- Luke 4:18

Jesus answered and said to them, "Go and tell John the things you have seen and heard: that the blind see, the lame walk, the lepers *are cleansed, the deaf hear, the dead are raised, **the poor have the gospel preached to them.** And blessed is he who is not offended because of Me."*

- Luke 7:22-23

"SO, WHAT WAS THE GOSPEL THAT WAS PREACHED TO THE JEWS ENSLAVED EGYPT?"

It was the gospel of milk and honey!!

And the Lord said:

*"I have surely seen the oppression of My people who are in Egypt, and have heard their cry because of their taskmasters, for I know their sorrows. So I have come down to deliver them out of the hand of the Egyptians, and to bring them up from that land to a good and large land, **to a land flowing with milk and honey...***

- Exodus 3:7-8

The promise of inheriting a land flowing with milk and honey *(the Promise Land)* was the hope of the children of Israel. It was this promise that kept them going as they wandered forty years in the wilderness, after their spectacular exodus from Egypt. The term *'flowing with milk and honey'* is used particularly for a land of abundant supply and unbridled opulence.

When the children of Israel finally reached the Promise Land, Moses sent out spies to scout the land. To prove that the land was, indeed, *flowing with milk and honey*, they brought back a cluster of grapes so big it had to be carried on a pole between two men! They also brought back pomegranates and figs. Not only was the land agriculturally rich, but it was also rich in minerals and precious metals.

*For the Lord your God is bringing you into a good land, a land of brooks of water, of fountains and springs, that flow out of valleys and hills; a land of wheat and barley, of vines and fig trees and pomegranates, a land of olive oil and honey; **a land in which you will eat bread without scarcity, in which you will lack nothing;** a land whose stones are iron and out of whose hills you can dig copper.*

- Deuteronomy 8:7-9

Deuteronomy 8 goes on to explain that in this lavish land, in which they would want for nothing, they would:

• Eat until they are full.
• Build beautiful houses and dwell in them.
• Increase their flocks and herds.
• Increase their gold and silver.
• Increase all that they have.

Therefore, the gospel preached to those held captive in Egypt was, indeed, *the gospel of prosperity,* preached by Christ as *the gospel of the Kingdom.* It was the good news of deliverance from a system of lack and limitation into a realm of prosperity and abundance.

CHAPTER 17

DIVINE REST

---◆---

"For if Joshua had given them rest, then He would not afterward have spoken of another day. There remains therefore a rest for the people of God"

THE MENTAL TERRITORY OF PEACE AND PROSPERITY

Although the children of Israel entered the Promise Land and prospered in the manner God said they would, their hardened hearts and relentless disobedience caused them to miss out on what God *really* had in store. The land they inhabited was only the physical equivalent of a far greater realm: **the mental territory of peace, victory, and prosperity.** In this realm, they would experience *'good success,'* the result of placing mind before matter. They would also experience deliverance from toil and labor, embracing an attitude to life exemplified by what the Bible calls *God's rest.*

*Today, if you will hear His voice: "Do not harden your hearts, as in the rebellion, as in the day of trial in the wilderness, when your fathers tested Me; They tried Me, though they saw My work. For forty years I was grieved with that generation, And said, 'It is a people who **go astray in their hearts,** And **they do not know My ways.'** So I swore in My wrath, **'They shall not enter My rest.'** "*

- Psalm 95:7-11

From the foundation of the world, God created everything that was to be manifested. This, He did, in six *'spiritual'* days and then *rested* on the seventh day. This is *'the rest'* God wants His children to enter into - **the assurance of His *finished* works.** God's rest encapsulates the peace of knowing that everything that pertains to your life and destiny has already been planned with an expected victorious end *(Jeremiah 29:11 KJV)*. Every hurdle has been overcome, every problem has been solved, and the best possible outcome has already been achieved.

Christ, Himself, rested in the assurance of what God had *predestined* for His life, even during the various times the Jews attempted to arrest or kill him! Such as when He was teaching in the synagogue, conveying 'truth' that struck a nerve with those who were listening. In response, they mobbed Him and threw Him out of the city.

Full of murderous intent, they took Him to the edge of a cliff so that they might hurl Him headlong down the precipice. Yet He *passed right through the crowd and went on his way' (Luke 4: 24-30).*

"HOW WAS JESUS ABLE TO WALK AWAY FROM A CROWD SO INCENSED ON KILLING HIM?"

There is no record of either men or angels coming to His aid, nor did He have to fight to avoid an untimely death. The answer lies in the account given of other times where people tried to apprehend Him because of the things He said:

*Then the leaders tried to arrest him; but no one laid a hand on him, because **his time had not yet come.***

- John 7:30 NLT

Because Jesus was in God's rest, *nothing* could derail Him from what was predestined for His life. Therefore, He could not be killed by the angry mob because the hour and manner of His death had already been determined.

God has indeed predestined our lives with an *expected end* and has nothing but good for us. However, contrary to what many believe, predestination is a path you must *choose* to walk. It is not inevitable! By the act of your own free will, God wants you to enter into the *good life* He has in store for you by manifesting what He has already planned and *finished* for your life.

FINISHED WORKS

The concept of God's rest may seem confusing, especially as it seems He is always at work. The wonders of nature constantly reflect God's handiwork, and miracles still happen today as they did when the Bible was being penned. Many can testify that,

"The blind receive their sight, the lame walk, lepers are cleansed, the deaf hear, and the dead are raised up."

- Matthew 11:5

"SO HOW DO WE EXPLAIN THESE APPARENT 'ACTS OF GOD' THAT TAKES PLACE IN NATURE AND IN OUR LIVES?"

The answer lies in the *laws and systems*. God has put laws and systems in place that manifest His finished works. For example, there are laws governing the systems of the physical world, such as the weather, the orbit of the earth, seasons, how our bodies function, and much more. These laws are so precise and dependable that we can put a spaceship on Mars with pinpoint accuracy. None of these things require God to do any work because 'finished works' are manifested by applying laws and systems.

In like manner, there are spiritual or divine laws that govern spiritual systems. These are the laws that determine the *moments, situations, circumstances, and events* that impact our lives. Again, God does not have to do any work because *'the work'* is manifested through divine laws and systems. The only difference being that divine law functions through *the mind*, by faith.

DECREE A THING!

During their exodus from Egypt, the children of Israel witnessed the most spectacular miracles recorded in the Bible. They saw the Red Sea part, and they walked across it. They then saw it close behind them, destroying the Egyptian army that pursued them. They saw water flow from a rock when they were thirsty, and they even witnessed the sun and the moon stand still. Despite all that they witnessed, they did not understand 'God's ways' - *who searches the heart and gives to everyone according to the fruit of their doings (Jeremiah 17:10)*. They were also unaware of the contract between the Spirit of God and the heart of man. A divine contract, giving men and women the authority to - *'Decree a thing'* with the expectation that it will be *established (Job 22:28)*. Had they realized that this contract exemplified the law of their being, they would know that,

*Whosoever says to this mountain, 'Be removed and be cast into the sea,' and does not doubt in his heart, **but believes that those things he says will be done, he will have whatever he says.***

- Mark 11:23

Unfortunately, they were blind to the truth of who they were! As a result, they failed to see that all of these mighty *finished works of God* were *subject* to the will of man. The Red Sea parted when *Moses* stretched out his hand, and it was at *Joshua's* command that sun and moon stood still. Even more profound was the time when Amalek fought against the children of Israel. When Moses stood on a hill and kept his hands raised in the heat of the battle, **Israel prevailed**. However, when he lowered his hands, as his arms grew tired, **Amalek**

prevailed. In the end, Moses had to have his hands propped up to enable Israel to be victorious. This clearly demonstrates the direct correlation between the heart and the Spirit of God and that divine power is subject to man's command. Not only for mighty prophets like Elijah and Elisha, but for *all* who believe. No one exemplified this truth more than the woman with the issue of blood.

Now a certain woman had a flow of blood for twelve years, and had suffered many things from many physicians. She had spent all that she had and was no better, but rather grew worse. When she heard about Jesus, she came behind Him in the crowd and touched His garment. For she said,

*"If only I may touch His clothes, **I shall be made well.**"*

Immediately the fountain of her blood was dried up, and she felt in her body that she was healed of the affliction. And Jesus, immediately knowing in Himself that power had gone out of Him, turned around in the crowd and said, "Who touched My clothes?" But His disciples said to Him, "You see the multitude thronging You, and You say, "Who touched Me?"" And He looked around to see her who had done this thing. But the woman, fearing and trembling, knowing what had happened to her, came and fell down before Him and told Him the whole truth. And He said to her,

*"Daughter, **your faith has made you well.** Go in peace, and be healed of your affliction."*

- Mark 5:25-34

Never before in the annals of scripture had someone determined the precise manner in which they would be healed without the knowledge or consent of a Prophet or Priest. However, although classed as an untouchable, this courageous woman overcame the stigma of her disease and pressed through the crowd *(an offense that carried the penalty of death by stoning for someone in her condition)*. Imagine the focus and determination it took as she pressed past people who knew of her, people who despised her, people who felt she had no right to be there. Not to *beg* Jesus for what she needed, but instead, *receive* what *she said* she would have. This woman's experience highlights the promise of 'rest' available to those willing to put their faith in God so that His finished works can be manifested in their lives.

CHAPTER 18

MANIFESTING FINISHED WORKS

◆

"The Son can do nothing of Himself, but what He sees the Father do; for whatever He does, the Son also does in like manner"

God's rest is not an option but a command. Rather than living by the sweat of your brow, God wants you to rest in the assurance of His finished works. He wants you to adopt the attitude that you've already won! God desires for you to be delivered from the fear and uncertainty that comes with relying on *self,* so that you may live a life of purpose and *divine ease.* Hence, Jesus says,

"Come to Me, all you who labor and are heavy laden, **and I will give you rest.** *Take My yoke upon you and* **learn from Me,** *for I am gentle and lowly in heart, and you will find rest for your souls. For My yoke is easy and My burden is light."*

- Matthew 11:28-30

Jesus lived a life void of anxiety because He knew God's will for His life. He knew His assignment. He was a man of vision. He did nothing but manifest the finished works of His Father.

"The Son can do nothing of Himself, but what He sees the Father do; for whatever He does, the Son also does in like manner."

- John 5:19

As explained in chapter 13, Jesus' ability to see the Father's works was not by divine visitation or a burning bush. It was simply what He saw in His mind. I will say it again, *"Jesus was obedient to what He saw in His mind!"* All the miraculous things He did, emanated from what He saw His Father doing on the screen of His imagination. His entire life, in the physical world, was about manifesting the finished works of the Father.

> ## "Jesus was obedient to what He saw in His mind."

When Jesus encountered a man that was apparently blind from birth *(implying that the man may have been born without eyes)*, His disciples asked if the man's condition was due to his own sin or that of his parents. Jesus replied,

"Neither hath this man sinned, nor his parents: but that the works of God should be made manifest in him"

- John 9:3.

Many believe God made the man blind to demonstrate His power at an appointed time! However, this is far from true. God is *not* the cause of sickness and disease, nor does He inflict anyone with such things just to demonstrate His power. Jesus simply took the opportunity to manifest, *within the man*, the finished works of God. His statement about the *'works of God'* being manifested, could have applied to *anyone* He encountered suffering from an affliction.

It is important not to confine the finished works of God to bodily healing and deliverance. As Peter reveals, God's divine power has given us all things pertaining to *life and godliness (2 Peter 1:3)*. The life that Peter is referring to is *Zoe life*, often defined as, - The God-kind of life.

The God-kind of life is the absolute fullness of life. It is a life of wholeness with *nothing missing or broken*. It is also the life by which we partake in the richness of the divine nature, outlined by joy, peace, freedom, success, divine health, and wealth.

Jesus invites you to learn from Him so that you may manifest the works of God. As the Son only did what He saw the Father doing, you too must do the same by:

• Discovering what God has already done for you.
• Believing that it has already been done
• Manifesting what you see into physical reality.

Only then can we enter into the divine life of victory, joy, and abundance.

CHAPTER 19

THE GOOD THAT YOU DESIRE

*"For God is working in you, giving you the desire
and the power to do what pleases Him"*

I n this book, much has been mentioned about *having the good that one desires*. To the religious mind, this may seem greedy, self-centered, or even sacrilegious. However, when

> **Your salvation comes about from working Out what God is working in You.**

you understand what *your salvation* is, you will find that having the good that you desire has less to do with what *you* want and more to do with what God desires.

Although salvation is usually thought of in terms of redemption and eternal destiny, it mainly refers to victory over one's enemies *(physically or spiritually)*, health, preservation, and protection. Overall, salvation is deliverance from all that threatens us, whether the threat is external or even from our own erroneous thinking! More often than not, we can be our own worst enemy, making decisions resulting in missed opportunities and unfulfilled desires. What is life but the fulfillment of one's desires, for desire is the very make up of our souls.

That being said, God does not want your life to be derailed by erroneous thinking and selfish desires. He wants you to have a life where your desires are fulfilled according to His will—a purpose-driven life of vision and destiny. Therefore, rather than a one-size-fits-all formula, *your salvation* is a tailor-made solution for overcoming anything that impedes your ability to fulfill your God-given vision. Whether that be sickness, lack or even other people, God has made a way of deliverance, and it's all in you.

*Work out **your own salvation** with fear and trembling; for **it is God who works in you** both to will and to do for His good pleasure.*

- Philippians 2:12-13

Your salvation comes about from **working out what God is working in you**. It is the dynamic of manifesting what is most desirable and pleasing to God. Everything you need for deliverance and victory, whether in your finances, health, or relationships, hinges on your ability to manifest your God-given desires. Therefore, when I speak of you having the good you desire, I am talking about *manifesting your own salvation!*

As the good you desire pertains to your salvation, fulfilling your desires should not be taken lightly. The fact that you must do this with *'fear and trembling'* indicates the seriousness of the matter. As mentioned earlier, Christ is the true vine, and we are the branches. The life of the vine flows into the branches. As a branch, you are to express the vine's life by bearing fruit! The life of the vine is God's thoughts, and the fruit is the manifestation of such thoughts, experienced in your heart as the good that you desire.

Jesus said,

"Every branch in Me that does not bear fruit He [The Father] takes away!"

- John 15:2

He then said,

*"If you abide in Me, and My words abide in you, you will ask what you desire, and it shall be done for you. **By this My Father is glorified, that you bear much fruit; so you will be My disciples.**"*

- John 15:1-8

Therefore, you cannot afford to entertain any notion that it is selfish to pursue the desires of your heart. Through your union with Christ, your desires are the seed of His Word in your heart, to be manifested for your good and the good of others. It is only when you *bear fruit* in this way that you give glory to God and do what pleases Him. Not only that, **you can only be considered a disciple of Christ when you fulfill God's good pleasure by manifesting the good that you desire!**

If you abide in Me, and My words abide in you, you will ask what you desire, and it shall be done for you. **By this My Father is glorified, that you bear much fruit; so you will be My disciples.**

- John 15:7-8

You are the vessel by which the things of God are manifested, utilized, and enjoyed on the earth. Jesus said, *"All things the Father has, belong to the Me,"* and through your union with Christ, they also belong to you.

CHAPTER 20

HOW GOOD DO YOU WANT GOD TO BE?

"Love your neighbor as yourself"

GOD IS GOOD! If you move in Charismatic or Pentecostal circles, you undoubtedly would have heard this statement on numerous occasions, rapturously followed by -

"ALL THE TIME!" God is good all the time, goodness expressed by success, joy, freedom, peace, prosperity, health, and wealth.

The question is,

"HOW 'GOOD' DO YOU WANT GOD TO BE - TO YOU?"

"DO YOU EVEN BELIEVE HE CAN BE GOOD TO YOU AS MUCH AS HE APPEARS TO BE TO OTHERS?"

"OR DO YOU THINK GOD HAS FAVORITES, HIS SPECIAL 'ANOINTED ONES' WHO SEEM TO GET ALL THE BLESSINGS?"

Although an argument can be made that God's love seems to shine brighter in some than in others, the truth is, *you* determine how good God can be to you! God is not a respecter of persons, and therefore, His goodness is available to all. However, the key to determining God's goodness in your life lies in two of the Bible's greatest commandments.

LOVE THE LORD YOUR GOD

A lawyer, asked Jesus a question, testing Him, and saying, "Teacher, which is the great commandment in the law?" Jesus said to him,

" 'You shall love the Lord your God with all your heart, with all your soul, and with all your mind.' This is the first and great commandment. And the second is like it:

'You shall love your neighbor as yourself.'

On these two commandments hang all the Law and the Prophets."

- Matthew 22:35-40

In our quest to *unlock* more of God's goodness, let us begin with this question;

"IF WE ARE TO LOVE THE LORD WITH ALL OUR HEART, SOUL, AND MIND AND THEN LOVE OUR NEIGHBOR AS WE LOVE OURSELVES, AT WHAT POINT DO WE LOVE OURSELVES?"

Between the two great commandments, there does not seem to be an opportunity to love oneself. So, how can we be expected to love our neighbor *as ourselves?* It would seem that the two greatest commandments, upon which the law and the Prophets hang, are, in fact, an oxymoron. However, given that God is not a God of confusion or contradiction, we are left with the only possible answer to this dilemma.

'TO LOVE GOD IS TO LOVE ONESELF!'

You can only love the Lord, your God, with all your heart, soul, and mind *by loving yourself.* Once you have loved God in this way, then you can love your neighbor as yourself.

If the notion of loving God through loving yourself seems selfish or egotistical, it is only because you see yourself as *separate* from God. As explained, mankind is the visible expression of the invisible God. **We were created to be the person God sees when He looks in the mirror!**

Therefore, you cannot love God apart from the person you can see. That was the great truth John taught when he wrote,

If someone says, "I love God," and hates his brother, he is a liar; **for he who does not love his brother whom he has seen, how can he love God whom he has not seen?** *And this commandment we have from Him: that he who loves God must love his brother also.*

- 1 John 4:20-21

You cannot love God, whom you have not seen, without loving the people you can see. You may hold some emotional attachment to the invisible God, but it is only counted as love when those emotions are directed to those He embodies - *and that begins with yourself!* When Jesus told the lawyers the *'greatest command,'* he quoted the latter part of a scripture verse they would have been intimately familiar with. It is essential to understand the earlier part of this scripture as it is the context and premise by which the greatest commandment was made.

ONENESS

"Hear, O Israel: The Lord our God, the Lord is one! You shall love the Lord your God with all your heart, with all your soul, and with all your strength."

- Deuteronomy 6:4-5

'Hear, O Israel: The Lord our God, the Lord is one,' is part of the Jewish prayer known as *'The Shema.'* The Shema is the most sacred text in the Jewish faith, declaring the *oneness of God.* However, where the Jews

interpret oneness as one sole entity, New Testament scripture clearly reveals that the oneness of God is the oneness of *multiple persons* in the Godhead, consisting of the Father, The Son, and The Holy Spirit - **The Trinity**. Further evidence of the triune God, or multiple persons in the Godhead, can be found in the Shema when we look at the Hebrew words for *'God is one Lord.'*

'Elohiym echad Jehovah'

The Hebrew word, *Elohiym*, translated in English as God, is *plural*. It is plural because it speaks of the plurality or expressions of God. That is why the word Elohiym is used to denote divine ones, rulers, judges, and gods. Most notably, Elohiym was the word used in Psalm 82:6 concerning God calling man *'gods.'*

"I said, You are gods [Elohiym] and children of the most high."

To clarify, Elohiym does not denote multiple Gods, but the same God expressed as many entities. God's children are gods not in of themselves, but through their *union* with Him. The Bible also makes it clear that anyone who is joined to the Lord is ONE SPIRIT *(1 Corinthians 6:17)*. As such, our oneness with God can be likened to the administration of the gifts of the Spirit described by the Apostle Paul:

*There are diversities of gifts, **but the same Spirit.***
*There are differences of ministries, **but the same Lord.***
And there are diversities of activities,
but it is the same God who works all in all.

-1 Corinthians 12:4-6

In Christ, we are all *'gifts of the Spirit.'* Our gifts, talents, skills, passions and brilliance are but the activities of the same Spirit who works all, in all, according to His own good purposes. Hence Paul urges us to keep the *unity of the Spirit* in the bond of peace. For there is,

• One body
• One Spirit,
• One hope,
• One Lord,
• One faith,
• One baptism,
• One God and Father of all...
...who is above all, and through all, **and in you all** (Ephesians 4:4-6).

God is a God of oneness, with Himself and His children. Therefore, it is in the context of oneness with God, you are to love Him, and that first requires you to love yourself! To transliterate John's point,

> 'YOU CANNOT LOVE GOD
> WHOM YOU HAVE NOT SEEN
> BUT HATE THE PERSON YOU SEE
> IN THE MIRROR.'

GOD-IN-YOU

Over the past millennia, Christianity has done more to promote the idea of sin-based unworthiness than any other entity. This, despite the fact that *Christ has nailed our sins to the cross*, and God chose to *remember our sins no more (Hebrews 8:12)*. Christianity has also taught many to

> **Low self-worth and self-harm is a violation of God's greatest commandment.**

put others before themselves. While the latter is admirable and needful in certain situations, it also makes you a target for abuse.

God's greatest command requires you to love the Lord *your God* by loving yourself. I emphasize *'Your God'* because I am actually referring to **GOD-IN-YOU**. GOD-IN-YOU is no less a God than He is anywhere else. Still, many in the church give more honor and reverence to a God in the sky. They also have more faith in what God does through pastors, prophets, and evangelists than what the same Lord is willing to do through and within them.

Somehow the church has woefully overlooked God's ultimate plan. A plan so fundamentally important that it was shrouded in secrecy from the beginning of time, only to be revealed and made manifest to the saints. This mysterious plan, which encompasses the fullness of God's glory, is this:

CHRIST-IN-YOU, THE HOPE OF GLORY
(Colossians 1:26-27)

Unfortunately, the magnitude of what it is to have Christ in you has been diminished by the constant bombardment of sin-based unworthiness projected from the pulpit of many churches. Unworthiness [low self-worth, poor self-image] causes you to value others above yourself, and sin-consciousness [guilt, iniquity] separates you from *your* God [God-in-you]. We will do well to understand Isaiah's cry:

Behold, the Lord's hand is not shortened, that it cannot save; neither his ear heavy, that it cannot hear: **But your iniquities have separated between you and your God, and your sins have hid his face from you,** *that he will not hear.*

- Isaiah 59:1-2

It is important to note that sin-consciousness does not hide *your* face from God. Instead, it hides *God's face* from you. A person's face is their identity, and, in Christ, **God's face is your identity!** Therefore, what you say about yourself, you say about God. To think, feel, or say that you are unworthy is to say God is unworthy. It is important that, like the prodigal son, you *'come to yourself,'* remembering where you came from and who you are!

• You were created in God's image.
• You are the visible image of the invisible God.
• You are the temple of God.
• You are God's chosen habitation.

Therefore, you should have a greater reverence for GOD-IN-YOU than any perception or concept of God outside of you. That can only be expressed by the love that you give to yourself. Oneness with God is epitomized by Christ being your *Ultimate Self.* When you understand your union with Him, you will realize that the greatest commandment of all is to *'Love Thyself,'* because,

Self-love is God-love.

The greatest commandments upon which the law and the Prophets hang, can be transliterated as:

1. Love GOD-IN-YOU by loving yourself.
2. Love your brothers and sisters as you love GOD-IN-YOU.

There are many situations where you should put others before yourself, but not at the cost of *violating* the greatest command. Allowing yourself to be abused is a violation of the greatest commandment. Low self-worth and self-harm are a violation of the greatest commandment.

- Value God by valuing yourself.
- Honor God by honoring yourself.
- Love God by loving yourself.

That is how you exercise your oneness with God.

THE ROYAL LAW

Once you have learned to love God by loving yourself, your love for God is made complete by *loving your neighbor as yourself.* This is the second great command which encompasses the first command, for the second cannot be fulfilled without the first. That is why James called the second law 'The Royal Law.'

If you really fulfill the royal law according to the Scripture, "You shall love your neighbor as yourself," you do well; but if you show partiality, you commit sin, and are convicted by the law as transgressors.

- James 2:8-9

The Royal Law is stated in the context of showing undue favoritism to others, especially with regard to how the poor were treated.

My brethren, do not hold the faith of our Lord Jesus Christ, the Lord of glory, with partiality. For if there should come into your assembly a man with gold rings, in fine apparel, and there should also come in a poor man in filthy clothes, and you pay attention to the one wearing the fine clothes and say to him, "You sit here in a good place," and say to the poor man, "You stand there," or, "Sit here at my footstool," have you not shown partiality among yourselves, and become judges with evil thoughts?

- James 1:4

Showing undue respect or treating others according to their financial status is a grave violation of the Royal Law. When you love others as yourselves, you are, in essence, loving **GOD-IN-THEM**. Therefore, not only are you doing someone a disservice when you treat them poorly, but you are also disrespecting God. You will do well to heed the words of Jesus when He spoke of how He will judge the world:

"When the Son of Man comes in His glory, and all the holy angels with Him, then He will sit on the throne of His glory. All the nations will be gathered before Him, and He will separate them one from another, as a shepherd divides his sheep from the goats. And He will set the sheep on His right hand, but the goats on the left.'

*Then the King will say to those on His right hand, 'Come, you blessed of My Father, inherit the kingdom prepared for you from the foundation of the world: for **I was hungry and you gave Me*** *food; I was thirsty and you gave Me drink; I was a stranger and you took Me in; I was naked and you clothed Me; I was sick and you visited Me; I was in prison and you came to Me.'*

*Then the righteous will answer Him, saying, 'Lord, when did we see You hungry and feed You, or thirsty and give You drink? When did we see You a stranger and take You in, or naked and clothe You? Or when did we see You sick, or in prison, and come to You?' And the King will answer and say to them, **'Assuredly, I say to you, inasmuch as you did it to one of the least of these My brethren, you did it to Me.'"***

- Matthew 25:31-40

Notice that *all nations* are gathered before Christ. Despite all the laws and doctrines that man finds salvation in, the only law that determines whether one inherits the Kingdom or not is The Royal Law. To love your fellow brothers and sisters is to love GOD-IN-THEM. To mistreat your brothers and sisters is to mistreat God. That is why the mark of a great leader is revealed by how they treat those who can do nothing for them!

BE GOOD TO GOD

Returning to the question of how good you want God to be, the answer lies in how good *you* want to be to God! If loving God is loving you, then *being good to yourself* is being good to God. Jesus said the Father is glorified when we bear fruit. In other words, we honor God when we manifest the fruit of His thoughts - that being, love, joy, peace, freedom, success, health, and wealth. There are numerous times where the Bible reminds us that,

'The earth is the Lord's and everything in it.' The gold is His; the silver is His, the cattle on a thousand hills are His (Haggai 2:8) (Psalm 50:10).

However, God is Spirit. What use could God have for material wealth if not through the enjoyment of those He inhabits. In that sense, God enjoys *your joy* of having *His goodness* in your life. Therefore, when you deprive yourself of His goodness, you deprive God of the *experience* of enjoying His goodness. When you shun prosperity, you deny God the joy of having that which belongs to Him. **You must realize that you and God are on life's journey together.** You take away from Him what *you believe* you and others should not have.

Place no limits on God's goodness in your life, for it is His good pleasure to give you *exceedingly abundantly above what you ask or think.* The joy of the Lord is your strength, so, therefore, your strength is His joy!

Do not let anything or anyone stop you from taking possession of the good that God wants you to have. The more of His goodness you manifest in your life, the more glory and joy you give to Him.

Love God by loving yourself. Do not deprive Him of the good that He wants you to enjoy. If God's love seems to shine more in the lives of others than it does in yours, it is only because He is enjoying life more in them than in you!

CHAPTER 21

YOUR DIVINE IDENTITY DEMANDS FOR YOU TO RICH

◆

"Clothe him in the best robe, put a ring on his hand and shoes on his feet"

I recently had the pleasure of re-watching *'Coming to America,'* the iconic movie from the '80s, starring Eddie Murphy and Arsenio Hall. Murphy plays Prince Akeem

Joffer, the crown prince of the fictional African nation of Zamunda, who travels to the USA in the hope of finding his Queen. In order to attract a woman who will love him for himself and not for his immense wealth, Prince Akeem and his personal aide, Semmi, rent a squalid tenement in Queens, New York, under the guise of poor foreign students. After a while, Semmi grows tired of this impoverished lifestyle. Against the Prince's approval, he secretly sends a telegram to Akeem's father, King Jaffe Joffer, requesting a *'cool $1Million'* because they were in dire straits! As the King was unaware of his son's plan to live in such poor conditions, he grew concerned. He decided to travel to America in person to bring his son home. When he arrives at Akeem's apartment, he discovers, to his horror, that his son was *'At work!!'* In his anger, he accosts Semmi and reprimands him for not taking better care of his son. As punishment, the King orders Semmi to confine himself to his *royal suite* at the Waldorf Astoria. Although he was suitably dressed, by anyone's standards, the King orders his aides to give Semmi a thorough bath and to clothe him in decent attire! Unable to hide his joy, Semmi cries,

"Oh, thank you, your Royal Majesty!"

King Jaffe's reaction towards seeing his beloved son living below his privilege somewhat reminds me of the loving father in Jesus' parable of the prodigal son. He, too, was a man of great wealth, and upon seeing his son in the distance, returning home barefoot, dirty and in rags, rushed out and kissed him. Having wasted his inheritance on wild and excessive living, his son had fallen on hard times. Reduced to feeding pigs and perishing with hunger, *he came to himself* and decided to return home to his father. Believing he was no longer worthy of being called his son, he hinged his hopes on his father being merciful enough to hire him as one of his servants. However, his cry of *unworthiness* fell on 'deaf ears,' and his father ordered his servants to clothe him in the best robe, put a ring on his hand and shoes on his feet *(Luke 15:11-22)*. This act, however, signified much more than a change of attire. It was the ancient custom of clothing someone in wealth and power. The same thing Pharoah did when he made Joseph ruler over all Egypt.

And Pharaoh said to Joseph, "See, I have set you over all the land of Egypt." Then Pharaoh took his signet ring off his hand and put it on Joseph's hand; and he clothed him in garments of fine linen and put a gold chain around his neck.

- Genesis 41:41-42

In clothing his son with wealth and power, the father restored his son's dignity, inheritance, and identity.

Like the prodigal son, your divine identity demands for you to be rich! God has ignored your cries of unworthiness and has decreed that you be clothed with wealth and power. As with the proud and noble King of Zamunda, the Most-High God does not want you to live below your privilege. **You are royalty!** Your life should be such that a small gesture from you elicits great joy, much like Semmi was overjoyed when he heard how he was to be punished!

Like the prodigal son, you don't have to do anything to get back into your Father's *'good graces'*, for Christ has already done that for you. God only desires for you to *'Come to Yourself.'* To be awakened by the revelation of **His Son in you** *(Galatians 1:15-16)*. To know and understand that you are more than what your circumstance depicts. You are, indeed, more than your color, more than your race, and more than how society sees you. Only when you realize that *'You Are More'* can God restore your dignity, inheritance, and divine identity. After all, the restoration of these things is what *salvation* is all about.

CHAPTER 22

HONOR THE LORD WITH WEALTH

"Honor the Lord with all your substance and with the first fruits of all thine increase"

With what has been said about our union with Christ and that God is glorified when we manifest *His goodness,* I can now shed light on divine law critical to your success but widely taught from the wrong perspective.

Honor the LORD with thy substance, and with the first fruits of all thine increase: So shall thy barns be filled with plenty, and thy presses shall burst out with new wine.

- Proverbs 3:9-10 KJV

Many prosperity preachers have taught that giving generously to the church *(or to a particular ministry)* is giving to God, and when you give to God in this way, He will make you rich! *"The more you give, the more you will receive!"* Other scriptures usually quoted in support of this are:

He who sows sparingly will also reap sparingly, and he who sows bountifully will also reap bountifully.

- 2 Corinthians 9:6

So let each one give as he purposes in his heart, not grudgingly or of necessity, for God loves a cheerful giver.

- 2 Corinthians 9:7

Unfortunately, this brand of teaching has led to the detriment and financial ruin of many, who, in good faith, gave almost all they had! Although *'giving'* is an essential principle in the Bible, many in the church faithfully pay their tithes and offerings but still struggle to make ends meet.

"SO WHY ARE SO MANY CHRISTIANS BROKE?"

"IS THE PROBLEM DOWN TO HOW MUCH OR LITTLE THEY GIVE?"

"IS IT BECAUSE THEY GIVE WITH THE WRONG OR SELFISH MOTIVES?"

Although the above could be considered contributing factors, the truth is,

'PUTTING MONEY IN AN OFFERING BOX WILL NOT SOLVE YOUR FINANCIAL PROBLEMS!'

Don't get me wrong! I am not saying you should refrain from giving to your church or any other charitable organization. On the contrary, it is imperative that you give financially to help others whenever it is needed. However, the financial abundance promised by honoring God with your substance and firstfruits has more to do with what you *receive* than what you give.

YOU MUST MANIFEST GOD'S WEALTH

To begin with, since the word *'substance'* is translated from the Hebrew word for wealth, Proverbs 3:9 actually requires you to *'Honor God with your wealth!'* As the Proverb presumes that *you already have wealth*, this immediately tells us that we do not honor God from a *position* of wealth rather than to *attain* wealth. This is because giving from a position of wealth is in keeping with the heart of God, whose very nature is to give to all liberally without reservation!

Indeed, God is the Ultimate Philanthropist, and so must His children be. Philanthropy is the divine calling of every believer and the ultimate purpose for becoming rich! Therefore, seek to manifest God's wealth in your life *first*. God has blessed you with every *spiritual* blessing *(Ephesians 1:3)*. However, spiritual blessings are of no use unless they are manifested into tangible things and material wealth. Therefore, honoring God requires you to *receive in your hands what He has put in your mind*.

THE FIRSTFRUITS PRINCIPLE

Secondly, we are to honor the Lord with the *firstfruits* of our increase. The concept of firstfruits is rooted in an era when people lived in an agrarian society. Harvest time was the most important time of the year because that was when the time and hard work the farmers invested into their crops began to pay dividends. God required His people to bring into His house, the firstfruits of their labor *(or business)* and all that was sown in the field. With the promise of their barns being filled with plenty, and their presses overflowing with new wine, the Hebrews saw these firstfruits as an **investment in their future.** It is important to note that the Bible does not dictate how much the firstfruits offering should be.

In the modern-day church, firstfruits have taken on a purely financial meaning and are deemed as an offering to be made above and beyond tithing. The firstfruit itself maybe:

• The first paycheck of a new job
• The first paycheck of the year
• The first portion of each subsequent paycheck
• The first portion earned from the sale of something
• The first portion of your bonus

- The first portion of a tax refund
- The first portion of each subsequent paycheck

…and so on and so forth.

The reasons stated for giving a first fruits offering also vary:

- To ensure God will bless the giver's plans for the new year
- To show sacrificial faith that God will provide
- To give thanks for God's provision
- To 'sow a seed' so that God will make the giver rich

Although the concept of the firstfruit is very much relevant to us today, there is nowhere in the New Testament where believers are required or even encouraged to give a firstfruits offering in a church service or wherever they assemble. As a matter-of-fact the firstfruit offering falls into an entirely different context from regular offerings and tithes. This is because in the New Testament, the term firstfruits takes on a *symbolic* meaning where we see Paul speaking of Christ as the *"first fruits of those who have fallen asleep" (1 Corinthians 15:20).* Therefore, firstfruits could well be of your time, money, or anything else of *personal* value. What hasn't changed is the fact that firstfruits is an investment in *your* future.

PAY YOURSELF FIRST

Although the concept of giving firstfruits to the Lord, or the *house* of the Lord, has been interpreted as giving to your local church, the truth is, '**You are the house of the Lord.**' That is the New Testament reality

> ### The most direct way to give a firstfruit offering to the Lord is to pay yourself first!

of what was symbolized in the old. The fundamental difference between the old covenant and the new is that the new covenant reflects the believer's union and oneness with Christ.

Therefore, the most direct way to give a firstfruit offering to the Lord is to **pay yourself first!** In so doing, you are investing in your own personal and spiritual growth, to the glory of God.

As previously mentioned, you should have a greater reverence for GOD-IN-YOU than any perception or concept of God outside of you. That can only be expressed by the love that you give to yourself.

Not only is paying yourself first a fundamental principle of personal finance, it also reflects the divine order of the greatest commandment and the Royal Law. Simply put, you must,

• Take care of yourself first, so you take care of others.
• Reward yourself first, so you can bless others.
• Invest in yourself first before investing in others.

At first glance, this may seem like an extremely selfish and egotistical act, and if you see yourself as *separate* from God, it could well be. However, when you are consciously aware that you are one with the Father, through Christ, taking care of yourself before taking care of others is a WIN-WIN way of living.

Love yourself first, *to the highest degree*, then love and care for others to the same degree. This, of course, must be done with the understanding that **loving you is loving God!**

The Bible does not specify what amount constitutes firstfruits because the firstfruit is a *personal offering* between you and God, agreed upon between you and God, that stays between you and God! When you give to God first, by paying, investing, and rewarding yourself first, your endeavors will be blessed! That is the overarching principle that applies to every facet of your life.

FIRSTFRUITS OF YOUR TIME

Without a doubt, Paul was the most successful of the New Testament apostles, doing more to spread the gospel than any other. Through Paul, the Spirit of God was able to convey spiritual wisdom Jesus refrained from sharing with His disciples because they lacked the spiritual maturity to receive it:

I still have many things to say to you, but you cannot bear them now. However, when He, the Spirit of truth, has come, He will guide you into all truth; for He will not speak on His own authority, but whatever He hears He will speak; and He will tell you things to come.

- John 16:12-13

HOW WAS PAUL ABLE TO KNOW AND DO SO MUCH MORE THAN THE DISCIPLES WHO SAT AND ATE WITH JESUS?

I believe it was due to the firstfruits principle of paying or investing in yourself first. **Paul's firstfruit offering was his time.** After his dramatic conversion on the road to Damascus, he spent three years of *exclusive* time with the Lord in the Arabian desert. It was in this time and solitude that he received the gospel through direct revelation from Christ.

But I make known to you, brethren, that the gospel which was preached by me is not according to man. For I neither received it from man, nor was I taught it, but it came through the revelation of Jesus Christ.

- Galatians 1:11-12

Paul spent quality time with God before doing what he was called to do - preaching the gospel to the Gentiles. Out of this firstfruit offering emerged the man through whom God would use to change the world.

Time is your most valuable asset. When given to God as a firstfruit offering, it pays a greater dividend than money. Therefore, give God your time by investing in your own personal and spiritual development. In so doing,

God is able to make all grace abound to you, so that having all sufficiency in all things at all times, you may abound in every good work.

- 2 Corinthians 9:8

CONCLUSION

To reiterate, your firstfruit giving should be done from a position of wealth rather than to attain wealth. You obviously cannot do that if you are apprehensive about becoming rich! Therefore, you should seek to:

- Manifest the wealth God has placed inside you
- Honor God by investing in yourself first
- Give God your best by becoming the best

In so doing, your future will be blessed, you will be a greater blessing to others, and you will always have the ability and the resources to do more good in the world.

CHAPTER 23

DON'T BE ON THE WAYSIDE

"There are some who trouble you and want to pervert the gospel of Christ"

A s previously explained, your salvation comes about from manifesting the thoughts and desires God sows in your heart *(subconscious mind)*. It is also how God seeks to give you what belongs to Him and clothe you with the wealth and power that befits your divine identity. To that aim, *God sent His word to prosper you*; and His word will not return on to Him until it has accomplished what it was sent to do.

So shall My word be that goes forth from My mouth; It shall not return to Me void, but it shall accomplish what I please, and it shall prosper in the thing for which I sent it.

- Isaiah 55:11

Your heart is *'the thing'* God's Word will prosper in, and His Word is the good news of the Kingdom. The good news of the Kingdom is the *'Seed'* that encapsulates all that pertains to restoring your wealth, influence, power, and identity in Christ. However, that seed can only bear fruit if the soil of your heart is *good*.

As identified in the parable of the sower, there are four spiritual conditions of the subconscious mind, and only *one* of those conditions will manifest divine thought.

The four spiritual conditions are:

The Wayside
- Spiritually ignorant or misguided

"When anyone hears the Word of the Kingdom, and does not understand it, then the wicked one comes and snatches away what was sown in his heart. This is he who received seed by the wayside."

- Matthew 13:19

Stony Places
– Superficial and shallow-minded

"He who received the seed on stony places, this is he who hears the Word and immediately receives it with joy; yet he has no root in himself, but endures only for a while. For when tribulation or persecution arises because of the Word, immediately he stumbles."

- Matthew 13:20-21

Among the thorns
– Easily distracted, materialistic, puts matter before mind

"Now he who received seed among the thorns is he who hears the Word, and the cares of this world and the deceitfulness of riches choke the Word, and he becomes unfruitful."

- Matthew 13:22

Good ground
– Full of faith, spiritual wisdom, and understanding

"He who received seed on the good ground is he who hears the Word and understands it, who indeed bears fruit and produces: some a hundredfold, some sixty, some thirty."

- Matthew 13:23

Out of the three conditions that do not produce fruit, *'The Wayside'* is the most insidious. While the others can be addressed by deepening your trust in God in order to:

• Develop the character, conviction, and fortitude to stand strong, even when others are trying to tear you down

And

• To put mind before matter so as not to be deceived by the influence of money...

"HOW DO YOU STOP SATAN FROM SNATCHING AWAY WHAT GOD SOWS IN YOUR HEART?"

Indeed, such a thing can only happen if you are already *predisposed* to the wiles of the enemy. Nothing makes you more vulnerable to Satan's schemes than your *ignorance*, especially if you fail to understand the paradigm and thinking of the Kingdom.

That said,

"IS THE WORD OF THE KINGDOM SO DIFFICULT TO UNDERSTAND?"

Apparently not, because the *'Stony heart'* person, who reflects those who are shallow-minded and lacking in spiritual fortitude, **received the Word with joy.** Even the *'Thorny heart'* individual, who is materialistic and puts *matter* before mind, must have first *received* the Word; otherwise, how could it have been choked? This point has profound implications because not only does the *'Word of the Kingdom,'* or even the *'Gospel of the Kingdom,'* appeal to people of faith but also to those who lead a superficial and materialistic lifestyle!

BUT IS THAT REALLY A SURPRISE?

After all, why wouldn't *anyone* be happy to hear that they can have success, joy, peace, freedom, good health, and wealth through the restoration of their divine identity?

SO, WHY WOULD THOSE ON THE WAYSIDE FAIL TO UNDERSTAND SUCH A MESSAGE?

The only possible answer is that 'Waysiders' *(misguided individuals predisposed to the wiles of the devil)* have been duped into embracing what Paul calls *'a different gospel.'* A *'poverty'* gospel that neither reflects the Jesus of the Bible or what He actually preached. The very thing Paul warns against.

For if he who comes preaches another Jesus whom we have not preached, or if you receive a different spirit which you have not received, or a different gospel which you have not accepted - you may well put up with it!

- 2 Corinthians 11:4

There are some who trouble you and want to pervert the gospel of Christ. But even if we, or an angel from heaven, preach any other gospel to you than what we have preached to you, let him be accursed.

- Galatians 1:7-8

THE GOSPEL OF THE KINGDOM IS GOOD NEWS TO THE POOR. There is no better news to the poor *(materially or spiritually)* than the restoration of their dignity, inheritance, and divine identity! To that end, *God sent His Word to prosper you.* Unfortunately, the widely accepted doctrine and virtues of poverty have created many Waysiders who reject the very notion of believers having wealth, success, influence, and power. To them, such things are deemed to be worldly, unspiritual, materialistic, and ungodly. Is it any wonder they fail to grasp *what others joyfully receive* or that Satan is able to snatch the very Word that was sown in their hearts!

In describing the spiritual condition of the *'Stony heart,'* Jesus gives the narrative of the inevitable persecution that would arise from receiving the Word of the Kingdom. If the Word sown does indeed relate to wealth, power, and successful living through Christ, then it stands to reason that the natural persecutors of those who receive the Word are those whose thinking is on the wayside.

'WAYSIDERS PERSECUTE THOSE WHO WANT TO ENTER THE KINGDOM WHILE AT THE SAME TIME ARE BEING PREVENTED FROM ENTERING THE KINGDOM.'

This destructive dynamic can only have been contrived by the insidious mind of Satan himself. Therefore, **the 'Waysider' must be set free** from being used as pawns, and everyone must know how to stand against Satan. To do this, we must first understand how Satan snatches away the Word sown in the heart. As mentioned, this can only happen to those already predisposed to the wiles of the enemy. What makes them so predisposed is the *paradigm* that they hold.

CHAPTER 24

GET BEHIND ME, SATAN!

———————◆———————

"Bring every thought into captivity to the obedience of Christ"

YOUR PARADIGM

Simply put, your paradigm is a set of subconscious beliefs that determine your actions and behavior. It is the lens through which you view the world and your perception of yourself. Colloquially put, your paradigm determines if your glass is *'half full or half empty.'* World-renowned author and speaker, Bob Proctor, defines your paradigm as,

'A mental program with almost exclusive control over your behavior.'

He also goes on to note that *all behavior is habitual.* This is key, as there are habits that pertain to success and those that pertain to being broke. Paradigms, therefore, govern your successes and your failures.

In his book, The Miseducation of the Negro *(one of the most important books ever written on education)*, Carter G. Woodson underscores the devastating effect of having the wrong paradigm.

> **"If you can control a man's thinking,**
> **you do not have to worry about his action.**
> **When you determine what a man shall think,**
> **you do not have to concern yourself about what he will do.**
> **If you make a man feel that he is inferior,**
> **you do not have to compel him to accept an inferior status,**
> **for he will seek it himself.**
> **If you make a man think that he is justly an outcast,**
> **you do not have to order him to the back door.**
> **He will go without being told; and if there is no back door,**
> **his very nature will demand one."**

For the most part, your paradigm did not originate with you. Instead, it is the accumulated inheritance of *generational beliefs*, often hardwired into the subconscious mind at an early age. As a result, many of the core beliefs that have become the guiding force of our lives originated from other people's habits, customs, and opinions.

This is especially so when it comes to the subject of money. That is why for many, the subject of money triggers a negative emotion, without a sound reason why. Rather than questioning the beliefs that cause such feelings, many choose to justify these feelings by hiding behind mental barriers disguised as morals, values, ethics, and even faith! Unless such paradigms are addressed, even if they consciously wanted to become successful, they will always have one foot on the accelerator and the other on the brake. Like Jesus said,

*"No one puts a piece from a new garment on an old one; otherwise the new makes a tear, and also the piece that was taken out of the new does not match the old. And **no one puts new wine into old wineskins;** or else the new wine will burst the wineskins and be spilled, and the wineskins will be ruined. But **new wine must be put into new wineskins,** and both are preserved."*

- Matthew 5:36-38

You cannot embrace a new life of prosperity and abundance with a poverty mindset. In short, **your financial freedom starts with a new paradigm!**

CAUSE AND EFFECT

As well as controlling your habitual behavior, paradigms also determine what you currently *attract* in your life. Although it may not seem possible, **your paradigm is the cause of the events in your life.** Your paradigm is the reason why you keep getting the same results, year in and year out, whether it be positive or negative. What you considered to be good or bad luck was the product of your paradigm. In that regard, there is no such thing as coincidence. Your life simply follows the GPS coordinates set out by your paradigm.

BLESSED OR CURSED

From a biblical perspective, paradigms closely correlate with *blessings and curses*. The Bible shows us that success in life has less to do with skills or talents and more to do with whether one is blessed or cursed. One need only read Deuteronomy 28 to see how the principle of the blessing or the curse encompasses every facet of life, - especially in the areas of health and wealth. I am not saying that skills are of little consequence. On the contrary, you should definitely commit to developing your skills and strive to be the best at what you do. However, many highly talented people are either broke or failing in key areas of their lives despite their best efforts. On the other hand, there are those who are less talented who just happen to be in the right place at the right time, making a connection with the right people who can open doors for them.

WHY DO SUCH THINGS HAPPEN TO ONE AND NOT TO THE OTHER?

Because of the universal principle of the blessing and the curse.

*"**Cursed is the man who trusts in man** and makes flesh his strength, whose heart departs from the Lord. For he shall be like a shrub in the desert, and shall not see when good comes, but shall inhabit the parched places in the wilderness, in a salt land which is not inhabited. **Blessed is the man who trusts in the Lord**, and whose*

hope is the Lord. For he shall be like a tree planted by the waters, which spreads out its roots by the river, and will not fear when heat comes; But its leaf will be green, and will not be anxious in the year of drought, nor will cease from yielding fruit."

- Jeremiah 17:5-8

The blessing correlates with the *divine paradigm*, the mind of Christ, that empowers one to prosper in all that they put their hand to. We see that in the life of Joseph, who was described as a prosperous man *even when he was a slave*. On the other hand, the curse correlates to paradigms that are contrary to divine thought, empowering those with such a mindset to fail or fall short of the life God wants them to enjoy.

Jesus' death on the cross broke the curse that mankind was under. However, if your paradigm does not change to God's way of thinking, you might as well still be under the curse. Hence, Paul urges us all to be **transformed by renewing our minds** - renewed to the paradigm of divine thought. In another place, Paul speaks of being renewed in the **spirit of your mind**, which is the biblical term for one's paradigm. Your paradigm, therefore, determines whether you are living a life that is blessed or one that is cursed!

God wants you to live a blessed life *(far above your circumstances)*, whereas Satan wants you to live under the curse *(far below your privilege and potential)*. To that aim, the devil seeks to contaminate your mind with his way of thinking. This brings us to the subject of how Satan is able to *snatch* the Word sown in the heart.

SNATCHING THE WORD

Unlike God, Satan is not omnipresent. He is a finite being who can only be in one place at a time. Therefore, it is implausible to think that he *personally* goes around snatching the Word from every Waysider on the planet. Instead, it is Satan's own thoughts that do the snatching. In the same way God and His thoughts are one, there is no difference between Satan and his thoughts. We too are the personification of our thoughts and if Satan's thoughts are impressed on our subconscious mind, they become part of our underlying beliefs. Once that happens, anything contrary to those underline beliefs will be rejected, *more so the Word of the Kingdom!*

Just as the act of snatching is quick and abrupt, Satan's thoughts in your mind will cause you to *instantly* dismiss anything that pertains to the abundant life God wants you to enjoy.

"BUT WHY WOULD ANY CHRISTIAN ACCEPT SATAN'S THOUGHTS? SURELY, ANY THOUGHT FROM HIM WOULD BE EVIL AND EASY TO REJECT."

You may be surprised to know that Satan's thoughts are not always overtly evil. As a matter-of-fact, as a fallen creature, his thinking is *very human*! Human reasoning reflects *'fallen thinking,'* which is contrary to the way God thinks. Hence, the Bible explains that God's thoughts are not our thoughts because they are *'higher thoughts' (Isaiah 55:8-9).* As previously explained, God does not say this to differentiate His thoughts from ours, but instead, highlight the depths to which our thoughts have fallen. Fallen thinking is the *native thinking* of Satan, whereas man was created to think like God.

The Bible also describes Satan as the *father of lies*, and the most effective lie is one **mixed with truth.** That is why you must know the truth of God's Word and avoid any departure from it. The more subtle the deviation, the more effective the lie. Even thoughts that seem good or well-meaning can be deemed Satanic if they are contrary to God's will. It is not without reason that the Bible warns us to guard our hearts with all diligence, and it is those *'well-meaning'* thoughts that we must be wary of the most. You simply cannot afford to adopt a casual approach to the thoughts you entertain, as that could be equivalent to entertaining Satan himself. Jesus was undoubtedly very aware of this fact, as demonstrated by His response to Peter's well-meaning thought.

From that time Jesus began to show to His disciples that He must go to Jerusalem, and suffer many things from the elders and chief priests and scribes, and be killed, and be raised the third day. Then Peter took Him aside and began to rebuke Him, saying,

"Far be it from You, Lord; this shall not happen to You!"

But He turned and said to Peter,

"Get behind Me, Satan! You are an offense to Me, for you are not mindful of the things of God, but the things of men."

- Matthew 16:21-23

At first glance, Jesus' response to Peter's concern about Him being killed may seem harsh. After all, he only said, *"This shall not happen to You,"* out of love for the Lord. But if for a moment, Jesus seriously entertained the thought of not dying on the cross, the ramifications for mankind would be catastrophic! Though well-meaning, Peter was expressing a *Satanic thought*. The Bible does not say that Satan possessed Peter, but what he said was contrary to God's plan. Therefore, although Peter spoke from a pure motive, he was conveying a word from Satan. As Satan and his thoughts are one, Jesus responded to what Peter said, as if He was addressing Satan in person. Turning His back to Peter, He said,

"GET BEHIND ME, SATAN!"

The Wuest New Testament Expanded Translation renders this as,

"Be gone under my authority, and keep on going, behind me, out of my sight, Satan!"

Jesus' response to Peter demonstrates the attitude and stance **we must take** when confronted with thoughts contrary to God's plan and the Word of the Kingdom, - no matter how *virtuous* they may seem. God sent His Word to prosper you. That is His desire for your life. Any thought or belief contrary to you prospering in every facet of your life stems from a paradigm rooted in Satan's fallen, *'human'* mind.

SATAN IS AFTER YOUR VISION

To reiterate, your paradigm has almost exclusive control over your life. The divine paradigm empowers you to live a blessed life of success, freedom, joy, peace, health, and wealth. A life where you will prosper at all that you put your hand to and express God's love through your generous giving. Satan, on the other hand, desires to bring you under the curse of his paradigm. As the Bible declares, when you are under the curse, **you will not see when good comes.**

*"Cursed is the man who trusts in man and makes flesh his strength, whose heart departs from the Lord. For he shall be like a shrub in the desert, **and shall not see when good comes,** but shall inhabit the parched places in the wilderness, in a salt land which is not inhabited."*

Satan is after your vision! He seeks to derail you from your God-given purpose. The well-meaning words he inspired Peter to say to Jesus, was in essence, an attack on His vision and mission. **Your vision is the blueprint of your life.** It is the medium through which God expresses His will. However, the ability to see and execute your vision can be undermined by the way you think. That is why Satan's battleground is in the mind. There are two key areas of thinking in which he focuses his attack:

Your health and Your wealth.

Without the support of health and wealth, you will not fulfill your vision. That is why Satan focuses his attack on these two areas. It is no wonder that when asked what area of life is most lacking, the answer from most people is nearly always health or money. These are the areas where people need help the most. Even more so, *(it seems)* in the lives of most Christians! The accumulative effect is that many Christians fall short of fulfilling their God-given vision! At best, they achieve a scaled-down, diluted, or miniature version of God's big dream!

No matter how 'purpose-driven' or vision orientated you are, you will always be *hobbling* through life without the support of health and wealth. Like someone who has to hobble because of a broken or injured foot, hobbling in life results from pain in one particular area, which throws your whole life out of balance and in a precarious state. That painful area is usually either in your health or your finances. Although we mainly encounter their physical counterpart, both wealth and health are states of mind!

RICH AND HEALTHY

> **It is just as much God's will for you to be healed in your finances as it is for you to be healed in your body.**

I have alluded to the fact that wealth is a paradigm but so too is health. In her best-selling book, *'Who Switched off My Brain,'* Dr. Caroline Leaf reveals from research that more than 87% to 98% of illnesses can be attributed to our *thought life.* Dr. Leaf also highlights the work of pioneering neuroscientist Dr. Candace Pert, who was called *"The Goddess of Neuroscience"* by her many fans. Dr. Candace Pert based much of her work on the theory that the body and mind function as a single psychosomatic network. Studies have shown that your thoughts trigger electrochemical reactions in your brain. These reactions cause the brain to release different types of chemicals according to the emotions of your thoughts. Depending on if these emotions are painful or pleasurable, the chemicals will either benefit or harm you. For example, pleasurable thoughts and emotions trigger the release of endorphins or *'feel-good chemicals.'*

On the other hand, painful thoughts and feelings can trigger the release of CRH, dubbed the *'negative emotion hormone.'* CRH, and other stress hormones that are subsequently released, can create conditions for a host of health problems that will manifest in the body.

Your thoughts, therefore, impact the health of your body, as well as the balance of your bank account! The devil would have us believe that sickness is just a *natural* part of life, but the truth is, nothing could be more unnatural. Unfortunately, humanity, as a whole, has accepted this lie, allowing sickness and disease to become an inevitable reality. Your identity demands for you to be rich and healthy. That is the *natural way* to live. However, it would take a *paradigm shift* for you to manifest that reality.

IN SICKNESS AND IN WEALTH

God does not want you to hobble through life. He wants you to live a purposeful life, enjoying divine health and wealth. To that aim, it is just as much His will for you to be healed in your finances as it is in your body. When the *'Woman with the issue of blood'* received healing in her body *(by her own determination)* Jesus said to her, *"Your faith has made you well."* But then, after that, He told her, *"Go in peace and be healed of your affliction!"*

"IF SHE WAS ALREADY MADE WELL BY HER FAITH, WHAT AFFLICTION WAS LEFT TO BE HEALED?"

The answer lies in the circumstances surrounding her healing.

She spent all that she had on many physicians and was now *broke!* Although she had the faith to obtain what she desired, she only went as far as her physical condition! Maybe, like many, she did not believe that God would restore her finances just as easily as He would restore her health. Fortunately for her, Jesus sees both bodily disease and financial lack as *'afflictions,'* and, therefore, took the opportunity to heal her of both. God is love. He cares about every facet of your life, not just the parts *you choose* to focus on. Therefore, your health and your wealth are of *equal* importance to Him. That is why He wishes *above all things* that you prosper and be in health *(3 John 1:2).* However, the key to living in perpetual health and wealth is to have a *prosperous* soul and mind.

BREAKING THE CURSE

Like leaven that affects the whole batch of dough, it only takes a small 'well-meaning' *thought-seed* from Satan to impact your entire life - propelling you in an endless cycle of defeat. This will certainly be the case when his thoughts become so entrenched in your subconscious mind; they are like fortresses or *strongholds* in your mind. Therefore, you will do well to heed Paul's instruction in dealing with particular trains of thought.

*For the weapons of our warfare are not carnal but mighty in God for pulling down strongholds, casting down **arguments** and **every high thing** that exalts itself against the knowledge of God, bringing every thought into captivity to the obedience of Christ, and being ready to punish all disobedience when your obedience is fulfilled.*

- 2 Corinthians 10:4-6

The arguments and *'high things'* Paul speaks of include those *self-righteous opinions* that seem to claim a higher moral ground than God's Word. These are the type of thoughts that must be pulled down and brought into captivity to the obedience of Christ. For instance, God sent His Word to prosper you! Therefore, in the same way Jesus brought down every thought seeking to come between Him and the cross, you too must bring down every *high-minded* thought, seeking to come between you and the prosperous life God wants you to have.

'Bring them *all* into captivity by executing your God-given authority over the author of such opinions.'

If you are a Kingdom-minded person, who is serious about having, not just personal wealth, but *generational wealth*, I am sure you have probably been confronted with these opinions or even criticized by Waysiders for desiring such wealth! These opinions are the usual response given by critics whenever it comes to the subject of wealth, prosperity, and having the good you desire.

I urge you not to allow yourself to be indicted by such opinions or made to feel guilty. Instead, follow Jesus' example and **command Satan to get behind you!!** *I will leave it to your discretion whether you choose to say this audibly or not.* Please note, in saying this command, you are speaking directly to Satan, not to the person under the influence of such opinions. In all things, you should remember who your real enemy is and seek to love and help your brothers and sisters.

Here are the most common statements deserving of the response - 'Get behind Me Satan' accompanied with a fitting rebuttal:

"Money is not everything"
- *"Get behind Me, Satan"*

Rebuttal: Working 8-12 hours a day, 5-6 days a week for money, is more representative of money being *'everything.'* Exchanging large amounts of your time for money, robs you of quality time with God, your spouse, and your family. Prosperity and financial freedom break the hold of money over you, allowing you to enjoy a life where money is not the central focus or need.

"Money is the root of all evil"
- *"Get behind Me, Satan!"*

Rebuttal: It is the *love* of money that is the root of all evil, not money itself. In many cases, it is the lack of money that causes division and strife. Money is a resource for goodness and empowerment when in the hands of those whose heart is towards God.

"You could have sold this and give to the poor"
- *"Get behind Me, Satan!"*

Rebuttal: Kingdom-minded individuals do not think in terms of lack. Like Christ, they view life through heaven's reality where the concept of lack and insufficiency does not exist. They know how to *'buy without money'* and manifest the good they desire from the Kingdom within. From this perspective, the statement, *"You could have sold this and give to the poor,"* is a foolish one because what I or any other believer have does not take away from what you can have!

Jesus only told the rich young ruler to sell what he had and give to the poor to enable him to enter into the realm of unlimited resources where he could have whatever he desired through trust in God.

"I just want to be comfortable and have enough for myself"
– "Get behind Me, Satan!"

Rebuttal: You have a responsibility to love your neighbor as yourself. *That is the Royal Law!* You cannot give to others and help them financially if you only have enough for yourself. You may embrace the idea of only wanting enough for yourself because you do not want to be greedy. However, not only is this a highly selfish and self-centered notion, but it is also worse than greed! Christ teaches us to give to those who ask you and lend, *hoping for nothing in return!* That is the nature of sons and daughters of God. You can't very well do that if you are always broke or only have enough for yourself.

These sentiments and more are no different from the false indignation displayed by Judas when he deemed the pouring of expensive oil on the head of Christ as a waste! They are all offensive terms, befitting the response - **"Get behind Me, Satan!"** You are more valuable to God than you can ever imagine. No amount of money on the planet can equal your worth. The King of Kings lives in you, through you, and *as you.* Therefore, wealth, riches, and power are the most appropriate things for you to have. No luxury item of any price can ever be wasted on you.

THE DECISION

---◆---

"This day I call the heavens and the earth as witnesses against you that I have set before you life and death"

To choose CHRIST is to choose LIFE.
Not an ordinary life but a rich trichotomy of
purpose, power, and destiny.

It is life at the highest level of living brought about
by the highest level of thinking.
Where dire circumstances can be changed
rather than be accepted.
Where impossibilities are merely the product of unbelief and
possibilities are subject to that which we choose to believe.
This is the *'everlasting life'* that God promised.

Everlasting life is the divine right of those who
dare to identify themselves with Christ.
The identity we lost in Adam but regained in Christ.
Everlasting life is not life after death but life despite death,
thanks to 'The One' who conquered death.

To choose Christ is to choose dominion.
You were created to have dominion on the earth.
That means you are supposed to have dominion over anything that
challenges your wellbeing and the wellbeing of others.
Whether it is in the area of your finances, health, career, relationships,
or spiritual growth, in Christ, you have dominion over them all.

When you choose Christ,
you will stand and shine in your uniqueness,
rather than sit on the bench of commonality.
Your uniqueness is the solution to the
needs of a specific set of people.
Your uniqueness is linked to the gifts and talents
that God meticulously wove into your divine make up.

We were all created with particular gifts and talents.
Some are discovered early in life, and others much later.
Often times we either sit on our talents or put them to improper use.
Only a few are fortunate enough to make a global impact with their
gift, and fewer still manage to find the true purpose of their gift.
Only in Christ do your gifts, talents, and uniqueness find their
purpose, bringing you to your place of influence.

In your place of influence you are strategically positioned to positively
impact the world, or to prevent the outcome of a dire situation.

That is your purpose.
That is your destiny.

We saw this in the life of Joseph, whose unique gifting was in
the area of dreams and the interpretation of them.
Although his gift led to him being sold into slavery by his brothers,
his gift also brought him to a place of influence.
It was his influence that saved the lives of millions from a dire
situation, *including the lives of his brothers.*
That was his destiny.

The world is waiting for your divine light to shine!
This can only be achieved in Christ,
where you discover your 'Ultimate Self.'

Lightning Source UK Ltd.
Milton Keynes UK
UKHW022354050422
401155UK00011B/406/J